HOW TO BE MORE IN

Edward de Bono invented the concept
A world-renowned writer and philosopher, he is the leading authority in the field of creative thinking and the direct teaching of thinking as a skill. In the decades since Dr de Bono introduced lateral thinking, the concept has become so entrenched in our language that it is used equally in physics lectures, television comedies or brainstorming sessions. His key contribution has been his understanding of the brain as self-organising system. His work spans generations, continents and belief systems, and is equally influential in the boardrooms of leading businesses such as Apple and British Airways as on the shelves of classrooms in rural Africa.

Dr de Bono has written more than sixty books, in forty languages, with people now teaching his methods world-wide. He has chaired a special summit of Nobel Prize laureates, had faculty appointments at the universities of Oxford, London, Cambridge and Harvard, and been hailed as one of the 250 people who have contributed most to mankind.

Dr de Bono's classic bestsellers include *Six Thinking Hats*, *Lateral Thinking*, *I Am Right You Are Wrong*, *How To Be More Interesting*, *Teach Yourself To Think*, *Teach Your Child How To Think*, and *Simplicity*.

www.debono.com

# HOW TO BE MORE INTERESTING

*Edward de Bono*

PENGUIN LIFE

AN IMPRINT OF

PENGUIN BOOKS

PENGUIN LIFE

UK | USA | Canada | Ireland | Australia
India | New Zealand | South Africa

Penguin Life is part of the Penguin Random House group of companies
whose addresses can be found at global.penguinrandomhouse.com.

First published by Viking 1997
Published in Penguin Books 1998
Published in Penguin Life 2016
002

Printed in Great Britain by Clays Ltd, St Ives plc

A CIP catalogue record for this book is available from the British Library

ISBN: 978-0-241-25752-4

www.greenpenguin.co.uk

# CONTENTS

# AUTHOR'S NOTE

There are many exercises in this book. You are strongly encouraged to do them. This is both to provide a pause so your brain can better absorb what you have just read, and also to emphasize the point that has been made.

The Exercises, which all appear on right-hand pages, are not at all difficult. Just note down your thoughts on a piece of paper.

The Suggested Answers, which all start on the page after the Exercises, are my own. I have done the exercises immediately after setting them up. So the thoughts given are from the top of my head – just as you would do the exercises. The sample answers are not the result of careful consideration. Almost all the exercises were set up randomly, so the exercises were just as new to me as they will be to you.

If you do not do the exercises you will only get half the value from this book.

The book is not a novel to be hurried through in order to 'see what happens'. Read through it slowly. Agree or disagree. Add your own experience and comments. Your intention should be to learn something from the book. If you learn nothing the fault could be either mine or yours. If you think you know it all already then the value of the book is to confirm your wisdom.

# PART 1

## INTRODUCTORY

## Foreword

This book is not about the interest that comes from celebrity, outstanding feats, unusual experience, an interesting job or special interest groups. The book is about the interest created by ordinary people living ordinary lives.

## Introduction

Being interesting is a 'skill' which can be developed. Being clever is not enough. Interest is not just an encyclopedia of facts but is full of possibilities and speculations.

## Playground of the Mind

It is in the playground of your mind that interest develops. It is the activity in your mind that elaborates around what is perceived. This is the 'richness' that is the basis of interest.

## FOREWORD

A beautiful face and a boring mind is boring, boring, boring.

A beautiful body with a boring mind is boring, boring, boring.

A fit and healthy body with a boring mind is boring, boring, boring.

A clever mind can also be boring, boring, boring.

I have known beautiful women who are very boring. I am sure there are beautiful women who are very interesting.

People spend a huge amount of time, trouble, care, worry and money on becoming or remaining beautiful. How much time do they spend on becoming interesting?

There are people who exercise and jog for hours every day in order to be fit and healthy. They watch their diets and carefully select what they eat. They load themselves up with vitamins and supplements. The result is often excellent. But how much time do they spend on developing an interesting mind?

Magazines and other publications have done a wonderful job in raising standards of attractiveness and health. People today are more visually attractive than they have ever been. Some of them are also more healthy than people have ever been. But all this is boring unless the beauty and health is accompanied by an interesting mind. So how much time do we spend on developing an interesting mind?

If you are indeed beautiful (and I use 'beauty' in the broadest sense) then you owe it to yourself to be interesting too. Otherwise all that beauty is wasted.

If you are not particularly beautiful then you had better work hard at being interesting.

All this seems obvious and reasonable – but there are two flaws in my argument.

If you are yourself a boring person do you notice that other people are boring? This is a very difficult question to answer. Suppose that a boring person does not notice that someone else is boring: then if you are content to live amongst boring people it should not much matter whether or not you are interesting. You would not notice how boring they were and they would not notice how boring you were.

I suspect, however, that even boring people notice how boring other people are. They can certainly notice when someone is interesting. So becoming interesting is not a waste of time even if most of your friends are content to be boring.

Is there perhaps the danger that, if you develop your ability to be interesting, you will notice even more than before how boring other people can be? If you develop a taste for the finest French wines, do you not notice the awfulness of lesser wines? I do not think the analogy holds, because in becoming more interesting you become more able to make other people interesting. It may be hard work but it can be done.

The second possible flaw in my argument is as follows. I stated that a beautiful body with a boring mind was indeed very boring. But many people have beautiful statues which they continue to enjoy even though those statues have even less of a mind than a boring person. That is true and if you are content to be treated as a statue or object or trophy then being interesting may not be important to you. Remember, however, that a statue is not expected to be interesting but people are expected to be interesting.

# Frames of Interest

I was having a drink with Buzz Aldrin and his charming wife Lois at the Four Seasons Hotel in Los Angeles. Whenever I looked at Buzz there was always that mental frame: 'This man has actually walked on the moon.' That is so powerful and so permanent a frame of interest that it outweighs everything else, but it so happens that Buzz is indeed very interesting in his own right – quite apart from that remarkable feat.

I used to know Peter Habler, the Austrian who was the first to climb to the top of Mount Everest without using oxygen. Again the frame of interest is very strong.

Clare Francis is a slight and very attractive woman who sailed single-handedly around the world. She then went on to write successful thrillers.

All these people were humble and not at all pretentious. Yet that powerful frame of interest makes them interesting.

Then there are people who have had interesting lives or done interesting things. A woman who lives for months with a tribe in the Amazon is going to be interesting. A nun who leaves the convent after ten years as a Reverend Mother is going to be interesting. Someone else might have been in the FBI or the Mafia or a spy in Moscow.

Someone may have an especially unusual job – like training fleas for a flea circus or being a wine taster. Another person might be notorious for having had eight wives in succession – or all at once.

Then there are the usual celebrities of film, television, etc. There is even derived celebrity: a girl who knew a man who once danced with Princess Diana.

It is difficult to separate curiosity from 'interest'. If you are 'interested' in that person then anything that person does becomes interesting. So fans would probably be interested in the colour of Tom Cruise's pyjamas.

I want to make clear that this book is not about frames of interest. If you want to become interesting by walking across the Sahara with two camels that is up to you – I shall say no more. If you want to become interesting by falling in love with a serial killer that is again up to you. Interesting jobs, interesting feats and interesting experiences can all make someone more interesting. But it is also possible to be interesting doing an ordinary job and living in an ordinary suburb. That is what this book is about.

## Special-interest Groups

There are racing fans who can discuss in minute detail the form of a particular horse. There are experts on fifteenth-century Italian art who can discuss with intense interest the development of the artist's palette. There are stock-market analysts who can discuss with great interest the imminent collapse of high-tech stocks. There are skilful gossips who can discuss the complex relationships of everyone at a certain party: who was with whom and who was deliberately not with whom.

Special-interest groups who play the game skilfully are always of interest to each other. That is also not what this book is about. If you wish to become an expert in champagne or post-modern architecture that could certainly make you a more interesting person. I do recommend the development of such special interests – but that is not what this book is about.

People belonging to special-interest groups are usually of interest to other people in that group. Occasionally a person with a special interest can also be of interest to others outside the special group. This all depends on a person's ability to make the subject interesting to others who do not already have the full background. Some people can do this while others cannot. The sort of 'interest' I shall be discussing in this book does not depend on having, acquiring or communicating knowledge of a specialized field.

## Very Ordinary

I fully acknowledge that all the types of 'interest' that I have outlined here are indeed a powerful way of becoming 'interesting'. The challenge is to see how an ordinary person leading an ordinary life can yet be interesting. It might be difficult to shine at basketball if you are not unusually tall. It might be difficult to shine at tennis if you do not have quick reflexes. But anyone can be more interesting if they pay attention to some of the things in this book. It is up to you.

# INTRODUCTION

I have known some very clever people who are not at all interesting.

Intelligence is like the horsepower of a car. Thinking is like the skill with which the car is driven. There may be a powerful car driven badly and a humble car driven well. Thinking is a skill which, like driving skill, can be taught and developed. That is why I am involved in various projects around the world for the direct teaching of thinking as a specific subject in schools. It is astonishing that the most fundamental of human skills should be neglected by education. It is assumed that thinking cannot be taught, but only learned as a by-product of some other subject. This is an absurd and old-fashioned view.

Some very clever people are only clever within their particular field. They have learned well the thinking idioms required in that field but have no generalizable thinking skills. When you talk to them they lay their thoughts before you just as if they were giving you a book to read. There is no interaction. You take it or leave it.

Some clever people are caught up in the 'intelligence trap'. This is a phrase I coined many years ago to describe why being intelligent was not enough. For example, many clever people believe that 'critical thinking' is enough. It is enough to be able to judge ('critical' comes from the Greek word *kritikos*, for judge). Such people are very ready to criticize but not so good at the generative thinking required to produce ideas. Another of the traditional nonsenses of education is to believe that teaching critical thinking is sufficient. Judgement is an important part of thinking just as the front left wheel of a car is an important part of the car. But a car needs more than a front left wheel. Teaching critical thinking is not enough.

A clever person might be interesting while explaining the intricacies of his or her particular field but is not necessarily interesting on other matters. Being interesting involves an interaction with the listener. It is what happens in the listener's mind that makes the listener interested. If the listener is not interested then, by definition, the speaker is not interesting.

An interesting conversation is very like jazz. There is improvisation. There is a to and fro. Themes are taken up and elaborated. Instruments talk to each other. There is always an onward flow. There is development. Sub-themes are taken up. The developments and interactions of jazz have their parallel in 'interest'. Just as a jazz musician develops skill in jazz so a person can develop skill in being interesting. This book is about the different components of that skill. The way we think and the way we express those thoughts will decide how interesting we are both to others and to ourselves.

## Facts and Figures

I have written this book very much as I would conduct a conversation. This is not a reference book for facts. There are times when I shall suggest a speculation for which a particular reader may know the exact answer. There are times when I may quote a figure which is in fact incorrect. As usual readers will rush to put me right.

What I shall put forward are the sort of remarks a person might make in an ordinary conversation and not in an examination thesis.

> 'I think . . .'

> 'I believe . . .'

> 'I seem to have read that . . .'

> 'I was once told . . .'

> 'This may not be so but . . .'

Of course, the truth is always of the utmost value but being interesting involves possibilities and speculation. If we did not dare to say something until we had double-checked the facts first then conversation would be most limited and uninteresting. We might as well just sit and read an encyclopedia.

The Italians have a very useful category which is not 'truth' but something which 'should be true'. A story is said to be *ben trovato*, which literally means 'well found'. If the story is interesting in its own right then it should be true. At the same time it is acknowledged that it may well not be true. There is nothing more dull than a pedant who insists you do not open your mouth unless you have completely checked out what you are going to say.

Provided you do not make false claims with competitive arrogance, the use of speculations and possibilities is a key part of being interesting.

Part of being interesting is the ability to 'play' with ideas. Solemn pomposity is the opposite of interest. Provided things are not claimed as absolute truth and provided they are not accepted as absolute truth, there is the fun of play. Young animals play in order to enjoy it and also to develop the life skills they will need. Playing with ideas is exactly the same.

# PLAYGROUND OF THE MIND

It is what happens in your mind that makes you interesting.

It is how you express what happens in your mind that makes you interesting.

It is what you cause to happen in the mind of a listener that makes you interesting.

Your mind is your playground. Your mind is your garden. You play as you wish. You grow what you wish. Just as an impresario puts on a stage show so you are the impresario of what goes on in your mind.

There is a huge difference between the mind and a camera. The camera just records passively what is placed in front of it. The human mind does very much more than record passively what is in front of it. Past experience is called upon; emotions, feelings and values are tapped; speculations and possibilities are opened up. It is the 'richness' of all this activity that is the source of 'interest'.

The cover of the book shows a spiral. This is because we 'create' interest as we spiral around a subject, moving ever wider to make further connections.

# EXERCISE 1

'A frog'

What is 'interesting' about a frog?

On a piece of paper write down the different things that are interesting about a frog. What are the lines of thought that open up?

---

Do not turn to the next page until you have attempted this exercise

## *Exercise 1: Suggested Answers*

What is interesting about 'a frog'?

. . . Why are young ladies encouraged to kiss a lot of frogs in the hope of one day finding the 'frog prince'? Why a 'frog' prince? Is it that ugly people look like frogs? Is it something to do with a French prince?

. . . Frogs compete in croaking the loudest in order to attract mates. This is competitive and gets attention. But what is the survival value? If the female frog mates with the loudest frog what survival value does this have? Perhaps being able to croak loudly is a direct indication of fitness and muscularity? Anyway, if the offspring are also loud croakers then they will also get mates. So the genes go forward.

. . . Frogs are amphibian and live equally well in water or on land. There are people who live in completely separate worlds and cope in both of them. Do we have to have single integrated lives?

. . . Movement by jumping. This is different from the kangaroo's movement by hopping. Is the jumping process energy-efficient? Or is it just that frogs have strong legs for swimming and then use them for jumping?

. . . How is it that the French are associated with eating frogs' legs? Did other cultures discover that delicacy? How are foods first discovered or tried? Is there a special type of frog that is more suitable for eating?

. . . Young frogs start off as tadpoles; a tadpole seems like a totally different creature that swims well but could not survive on land. Perhaps humans should think of children as totally different creatures and not as mini-adults?

. . . In South America some tribes obtain the deadly poison for their darts from frogs. If such frogs are poisonous to eat does this mean that those predators who eat frogs die out? Or do they learn their lesson by watching their frog-eating friends die? How did the frogs start developing the poison defence? How did the hunters first discover the power of the poison?

. . . There is a well-known story of a frog race (Talameda County?) but I cannot remember the author or the name of the place. Could frog racing, say on television, be a good gambling sport?

There are many more and many different places your mind may have gone in its elaboration around the simple subject of 'frog'. Some of these lines of thought might have required special knowledge. Others are questions and speculations. In some cases there is a transference of some aspect to human behaviour (living in two worlds). Any one of these ideas could be the starting-point for an extended line of thinking and discussion. For example, loud croaking as a basis for selecting a mate opens up the whole area of mate selection. Do the males just display and the females seek them out and do the choosing? Is it really like this with humans – even though it may appear otherwise?

The thinking habits and operations involved in this process of elaboration will be examined in separate sections later in this book. Why are some lines of thinking more interesting than others?

# EXERCISE 2

'A flower is red.'

What elaborations of 'interest' can you make around this simple statement? The exercise is similar to the preceding exercise. You may visualize a particular flower if you wish. Put down your thoughts on a piece of paper.

---

Do not turn to the next page until you have attempted this exercise

---

## *Exercise 2: Suggested Answers*

'A flower is red.'

... Life would be much duller if flowers did not have colours. But flowers did not develop colours just to amuse us. How many things can we enjoy which are there for a more practical purpose?

... Red is a very visible colour, so that the flower attracts bees and insects, which presumably help in pollination. Because red is a bright colour fire-engines are often painted red. But red is actually not easy to see at night. That is why some fire-engines are now being painted yellow, which is a better colour for visibility. Perhaps there could be stripes of yellow and red?

... Red as a colour is very much in favour with the Chinese. Why?

... Red was the colour pre-empted by the Communists. Different colours come to have different ideological or political values. Green is for ecology. Green is also for Islam. Green is also associated with Ireland. Pepsi-Cola is trying to get an association with blue. Afro-Americans are very sensitized to the use of 'black'.

... Can people 'own' colours?

... Flowers that wish to attract night insects are usually white. They also usually have a strong scent. Some roses also have strong scents. What role does the scent play? Is the scent an attractor from a distance because scents can be carried by the wind over long distances? Should humans think about 'distant attractors' as well as 'close-range attractors'?

... Can the pigment of flowers be extracted and used for painting?

... Are flowers competitive, with one colour doing better than others in attracting insects? Or do different colours attract different insects?

As with the previous exercise there is a mixture of speculations, questions, some knowledge and some transference to humans.

There are many other possible avenues of exploration. What about 'red roses for love'? What is the language of flowers? Is it the same in all cultures? In Japan it is very offensive to give white flowers because this signals a funeral.

What I have tried to do with these simple examples is to illustrate how it is up to your mind to elaborate ideas around a simple starting-point. It is like opening a small door in a high wall and suddenly finding yourself in a wonderful garden. This analogy is not quite exact because you discover a garden which is already there. With the mind, part of the elaboration is there but other parts have to be produced by the mind through such things as speculation and possibilities.

# EXERCISE 3

There are three groups of three words. All these were randomly obtained. In each group pick out the word which would be most 'interesting' to yourself. Explain why on a piece of paper. Then do the same exercise for 'other people'. The result may be the same or different.

yacht, chess, trampoline

mirror, leaf, sugar

island, whisper, trumpet

---

Do not turn to the next page until you have attempted this exercise

---

## Exercise 3: Suggested Answers

The main purpose of the exercise was to get you to examine the potential 'interest' of each word. Obviously, the choice of words will be very subjective.

My first choice would be 'trampoline'. Although there is very much more that could be thought about 'yacht' and 'chess', the interesting thing about a trampoline is that you get back the energy you put in. To me this is a very interesting concept. In how many situations does that happen? It also means that we can store energy and build it up (jumping higher and higher). Although the elaboration is not actually as 'rich' as with the other words, it is more interesting because more unusual. I suspect many people would choose 'yacht' because there is a lot of action and associations (America's Cup, etc.). Also the idea of using natural (wind) energy is indeed interesting.

My next choice would be 'mirror'. There is a fascination with mirrors. They show us how we are. Imagine a world without mirrors. We would be able to get some reflections from water and ordinary glass but would want to get ever better reflections. How do mirrors do it? Why is the person in the mirror shaving with the opposite hand? (The explanation is indeed fascinating.) I suspect most other people would also choose 'mirror' – unless they were trying to be deliberately different.

My next choice would be 'island'. That is a very personal choice because I love islands. I have a beautiful island in the lagoon in Venice. I like the separateness of islands. When you are on an island that becomes the whole world. The rest no longer matters. I think most other people would choose 'trumpet' because it opens up a wide range of elaboration: music, expression, emotions, triumph, military glory, Jericho, etc. Some might choose 'whisper' because there is always intrigue about whispering. What secret is being whispered? Why should others not hear?

The choice is indeed subjective and personal. The personal element always adds an extra bit of interest.

What I have sought to do in this section is to suggest, and to illustrate, that it is the activity in your own mind that provides the 'richness' that is the basis of interest. Why is something of interest to you? That is the first step. The second step is to make it of interest to someone else. For example, my personal interest in islands is not necessarily of interest to anyone else unless I can communicate that interest. Sometimes interest attaches to a subject, in which case communicating the interest is easy. At other times it is the way you approach and communicate your thinking about a subject that makes it interesting.

# PART 2

# THE BASIC OPERATIONS OF INTEREST

## Possibility

Opening up and exploring possibilities in the mind. Going beyond what is in front of you. The role of hypothesis and speculation.

## Alternatives

The deliberate generation of alternatives. Alternatives of explanation, action, ways of looking at things, etc. The importance of the 'fixed point'.

## Concepts

The fundamental importance of concepts to all thinking. Concept extraction as a source of interest.

## Run Forward in the Mind

Visualization, imagination and projection. Looking ahead, moment to moment, to see what follows and what happens next. Exploring forward in time.

## Connect and Link Up

The effort to make connections and to link up different matters. Skill at connecting things enlarges the field of interest. We are no longer limited to the immediate matters.

## Provocation

With provocation there may not be a reason for saying something until after it has been said. Provocations are the basis of creativity. Provocations open up new lines of thought.

## Attention-directing

Where do we direct our attention? Why do we direct attention? Attention either flows on or is directed. Directing attention creates the dance of attention that is central to interest.

## Alleys, Avenues and Themes

We choose to open up and to pursue avenues and alleys of interest. How do we notice them? Why do we choose them? Themes are very broad areas of attention.

## Clarify, List and Summarize

The need to express things simply and to communicate them well. The use of analogies and metaphors. The value of lists in clarifying thinking and providing attention points.

# POSSIBILITY

Almost everyone knows that 'possibility' is the most important word in the success of Western civilization – where it has been successful. Very few philosophers will tell you that. No university puts sufficient emphasis on the importance of possibility. Progress is supposed to come about through information, logic and truth seeking. Without possibility there would have been no success in science and technology.

Two thousand years ago Chinese technology was far ahead of Western technology. Had that progress continued, China would totally dominate the world today. But it did not continue. The Chinese never developed the 'possibility' system of the hypothesis. Their scholars were content to tie things up in description packages (like so much university work today). The scholars dominated and crippled China's development – which is why Mao had his Cultural Revolution.

Without the hypothesis there is no progress in science. Without the 'possibility' vision there is no progress in technology.

Possibility is very largely the basis of 'interest'. If we could only open our mouths to deliver encyclopedic facts we should largely remain silent. Interest would be confined to only those facts which were themselves interesting. It is possibility and speculation that can make anything interesting.

# EXERCISE 4

Why do llamas (the South America animal) have long necks? This also applies to vicunas and alpacas. We think we know why giraffes have long necks. The giraffes with the longer necks could reach leaves higher on the tree, so evolution favoured longer necks.

What are the 'possible' explanations? Why has evolution favoured llamas with long necks?

You may know the answer – if there is one. Otherwise write down some 'possible' explanations on a piece of paper.

Do not turn to the next page until you have attempted this exercise

## *Exercise 4: Suggested Answers*

Why do llamas have long necks? What are some possible explanations?

1. The same reason as for giraffes. They may be better able to reach leaves on trees or the tops of shrubs.

2. If you have long legs you need a long neck in order to graze comfortably. Otherwise you would have to kneel down to graze or have an elephant's trunk.

3. If you are grazing on a hillside then the long neck allows you to graze in a wider circle without having to shift your position. This applies equally on flat ground but shifting position on a hillside might be more tricky.

4. In long grass you cannot see ahead unless you have a long neck to raise the height of your eyes above the ground. This may be useful for ordinary life. It is most essential for the male llama to see where the females might be. Conversely the females with long necks are more easily spotted by the males and so mate more. (It is politically correct to say it might be exactly the other way around.)

5. A long neck may be easier for balancing when running over tricky ground.

There may be a perfectly sound explanation differing from any of the above. The exercise, however, is the generation of possibilities, not the parading of knowledge.

## **Opening Up**

Possibilities open up possibilities. This process of opening things up is the key to being interesting. Being dogmatic and always narrowing down to certainty is boring.

There is research to show that when girls are learning to read they use their brains in a way that is very different from the way in which boys use their brains. With girls many different areas of the brain are activated. With boys it is just one area (the Broca area). Why should this be so? We can 'speculate' and open up possibilities. We can imagine the female brain later in life. If the female is looking after young then any strange sound has to be identified because it could mean danger and the need to defend the young or to remove them. So 'meaning' has a scanning sense. Could it be this? Each possibility has to be scanned in order to identify what it might be. If the male is hunting, in an aggressive mood or in a mating mood, then meaning is much more 'focused'. There is one objective at a time.

Opening up possibilities is a matter of scanning within the mind.

# EXERCISE 5

In each of the following sentences there is one word missing (as shown by the dots). For each sentence insert a number of possible words that would make sense – for yourself or for others.

'I never . . . on Sundays.'

Men are much more . . . than women.

When telling a lie you should always . . .

(Note: in some cases more than one word may be used.)

---

Do not turn to the next page until you have attempted this exercise

---

## *Exercise 5: Suggested Answers*

I never drink on Sundays.
I never swear on Sundays.
I never get dressed on Sundays.
I never hate on Sundays.

Men are much more deceitful than women.
Men are much more romantic than women.
Men are much more practical than women.
Men are much more unreliable than women.

When telling a lie you should always smile.
When telling a lie you should always shout.
When telling a lie you should always stare.
When telling a lie you should always look away.

The exercise is more fun if the missing word does have some
relevance to opinions or people and is not just random.

## Levels

Where does 'possibility' fit in with truth and other matters?
There are a number of different levels.

CERTAIN: Absolutely definite. A confirmed fact. Truth
accepted by everyone.

ALMOST CERTAIN: You cannot be 100 per cent sure. When
you get up in the morning you cannot be sure you will be alive to
go to bed that evening. When you get into a car you might just
have an accident. But for all practical purposes you are certain.

PROBABLE: Something is likely. The balance of probability is
that it will happen. It is probable that there will be a McDonalds
in any big town. It is probable that if you insult someone they will
get offended.

POSSIBLE: It is 'possible'. This is much less than a probability and may even range down to 'just possible'. There does, however, have to be some real possibility.

FANCY: This is something you say or believe, not because you believe it is possible but because it serves some purpose such as enjoyment. The likelihood may be very low but you are not claiming real possibility. You may want to believe there is some magic fruit which if eaten can make you wise for ever. (More realistically, you could read my *Textbook of Wisdom*.)

FANTASY: There is no expectation whatever that something will happen or even be possible. There may be a fantasy that you could fly or be beamed up to a spaceship or have a date with your favourite celebrity. With fantasy anything goes.

It is important to note that 'possible' must have some element of logic or reality in it. We may have no means of knowing or checking if something is indeed true or even likely, but it is possible that it is true. A hypothesis in science is not a random guess.

In science we set out to see if the 'possibility' is indeed true. Where possibility is used as a base for 'interest', there are two levels of interest.

1. Could it be true?

2. What would result if it were true?

In a sense we explore the consequences of the possibility actually being a reality.

Possibility is only limited by imagination. As you make a conscious effort to open up and explore possibilities your imagination will get better and better. It is the pause to explore possibilities that matters. If you rush ahead without pausing then your imagination never gets a chance.

# EXERCISE 6

The shape shown here does not have an obvious definite meaning. What are the different possibilities? What might it represent?

Think of it at two levels:

A. What might it really represent?

B. What might it represent symbolically (if it was a deliberate work of art)?

---

Do not turn to the next page until you have attempted this exercise

---

## Exercise 6: Suggested Answers

A (real representation):

. . . an overhead view of a rat caught under a bucket with the tail
sticking out
. . . a new experimental type of kite
. . . a 'designer' frying-pan
. . . an overhead view of someone wearing a large coolie hat with
a pigtail flying out in the wind
. . . the track made by a drunken snail climbing out of a saucer of
paint
. . . a plain button with a loose thread.

B (deliberate and symbolic):

. . the path to a destination is never smooth.
. . . everything perfect has some tail of imperfection attached to
it.
. . . a curve can be complete as a circle or incomplete as a wave.
. . . we can only see the visible part. We do not know what else is
going on.
. . . is the circle a destination or a source? Is the wiggly line going
into the circle or coming out of it? Is something a beginning or
an end?
. . . the circle is unravelling into the line just as a knitted garment
might unravel. What happens when things start to come apart?

## Speculation

There is so much overlap between possibility, hypothesis and
speculation that they could all be treated as the same thing without
much loss. A hypothesis does fit the available evidence and you
do hope that it will prove to be correct. You work towards showing
that it is true. A speculation is weaker than a hypothesis. A
speculation is a possibility that you use in order to find some

evidence from which you may then form a hypothesis. There may be little or no evidence for a speculation. A speculation, as in the investment world, is really a gamble. Might it be so?

In the world of 'interest' speculations are fun because they are open to people who do not have special knowledge. A hypothesis is much more serious. The purpose of a speculation is to set off thinking in a certain direction.

Speculations must always be treated as speculations. There should be no attempt to claim them as truth or even as a hypothesis. Once this is accepted then it becomes possible to make interesting speculations.

Like a hypothesis, a speculation provides a frame through which we can look at a part of the world. Speculations add richness and interest to thinking and to conversation.

Why do fatter people seem to have a better sense of humour?
. . . because their relaxed enjoyment of life made them fatter in the first place.
. . . because their hormones are more in harmony.
. . . to protect their inner sadness.
. . . because laughter is their way of contributing and being liked.
. . . because they are not anxiously trying to maintain some image.
. . . because they laugh louder and are therefore more noticeable.
. . . because people expect fatter people to be happier and so notice it (self-fulfilling prophecy).

These are all speculations that get us thinking. As far as I know there is no evidence to suggest any one of them as a 'hypothesis'.

# EXERCISE 7

Some cultures write from the left-hand side of the page across to the right. Other cultures write from the right-hand side of the page across to the left-hand side. Why do you think this is? Try some speculation.

Do not turn to the next page until you have attempted this exercise

## *Exercise 7: Suggested Answers*

Here is one speculation. There may be a known answer. The purpose of the exercise is to try your own speculation. What is present here is my speculation and is not based on knowing the answer.

If you are right-handed and you write by making marks on a clay tablet, then you have to proceed from right-hand side to left-hand side because that is the only way you can push the marker into the clay. It is the only way you can exert pressure with the right hand.

If you write by laying pigment or dye on a surface then you proceed from left-hand side to right-hand side otherwise your own hand will smudge the pigment. It is also easier to lay down the pigment (with a pen or brush) by moving from left to right.

Middle-eastern cultures did seem to write by making marks on clay tablets, which may be why they now write from right to left.

## Mental Habits

Understanding the value of possibilities and deliberately searching for them can become a mental habit. It is a matter of pausing to explore possibilities.

Possibilities are a whole area of mental activity which lies between truth and total fantasy. It is a very rich area because for any one truth there are many possibilities.

At the same time there is a skill in exploring for possibilities and setting up speculations. The more 'reasonable' they are the more interesting they will be. Total, unrestricted fantasy may be amusing from time to time but it is not usually 'interesting'.

If you stick only to known 'truths' and facts then you are likely to be boring. Possibility is a major game to be played in the playground of the mind.

## ALTERNATIVES

Creativity is all about generating alternatives.

What are the alternative explanations?

What are the alternative courses of action?

What are the alternative choices?

What are the alternative ways of doing this?

What are the alternative ways of looking at this?

'Possibility' leads directly into alternatives. It is possibility that discovers, creates and designs the alternatives. Technically, alternative means 'one other' but in practice it now means many possibilities.

Alternatives are the best antidote to dogmatism and arrogance. 'Yes, that is one way of looking at it, but it is not the only one.' In science, proof is often no more than lack of imagination. We assume that A must cause B because we cannot imagine any other possibility. A good scientist imagines the alternative explanations and then tries to eliminate or check out each one. Arrogant people fasten on to the one view that suits their purposes and insist on its validity. Validity is enough.

There are times when several alternatives are equally valid. They may be parallel causes or contributory factors. Juvenile street crime may be caused by drugs, by family breakdown, by gang culture, by the influence of TV and by unemployment. It would be arrogant to insist on only one of these causes.

Alternatives are the best alternative to negativity. If you do not agree with someone then try to see why you do not agree.

1. It may be that you are dealing with different basic facts.

2. It may be that you are looking at a different part of the situation.

3. It may be that you are seeing things from a different point of view.

4. It may be that you are using different values.

5. It may be that your projection into the future is different.

With normal argument you would disagree immediately and then set out to argue the point. Instead you lay out the other person's point of view and then you lay out – in parallel – your own point of view. Very often both can co-exist because of different values or different information or different projections. Parallel thinking is much quicker and more powerful than argument. The Six Hats method of parallel thinking is now in use with many major corporations and other organizations around the world. It can reduce meeting times by up to 75 per cent. (See my books *Parallel Thinking* and *Six Thinking Hats*.)

Alternatives are part of the basic 'richness' of interest. It is obvious that not all alternatives are equally possible, equally valuable or equally practical. Interest lies both in generating the alternatives and then in examining them. A feast of alternatives provides an excellent mental meal.

Consider the simple equation $5 + 3 = 8$
There is no other possible answer.

Consider $8 = 3 + 5$

While this is certainly correct there are many, many possible answers.

$8 = 4 + 4$
$8 = 6 + 2$
$8 = 4 \times 2$
$8 = 12 - 4$

# EXERCISE 8

This is an exercise in generating alternatives.

You can use the numbers 3, 4, 5 as often as you wish. You can use the basic mathematical operations: plus, minus, division, multiplication. In how many different ways can you arrange the numbers to give the exact total of 30? Try at least four different ways.

---

Do not turn to the next page until you have attempted this exercise

## *Exercise 8: Suggested Answers*

$(3 \times 5) + (3 \times 5) = 30$

$4 \times 5 + 5 + 5 = 30$

$3 \times (4 + 5) + 3 = 30$

$5 \times (4 + 3) - 5 = 30$

With numbers you can easily check whether your alternative answer is correct. In most cases, an alternative is only an offered possibility.

In some cases it is possible to analyse out the different alternatives. This is a matter of 'discovering' the alternatives. In other cases the alternatives are subjective and depend entirely on your choice: on how you choose to look at something. There can also be 'designed' alternatives where you add something to the situation in order to design further alternatives.

# EXERCISE 9

This exercise depends on your choice of how to look at things.

A. There are eight randomly obtained words. Divide them into two groups of four in each group. Be clear about the basis for the grouping. If the basis is a concept put down the concept. Simple division into 'the first four' and 'the second four' is not acceptable.

B. You can exchange one of the words for any other word of your choice. Proceed as for (A).

In both (A) and (B) put down two alternative divisions.

snake, bath, gym, dance, soldier, soup, crane, bridge.

---

Do not turn to the next page until you have attempted this exercise

---

## *Exercise 9: Suggested Answers*

A:

Four contain the letter 'a' and four do not:
snake, bath, dance, crane  / /  gym, soldier, soup, bridge

Four imply a type of human activity and four do not:
bath, gym, dance, soldier  / /  snake, soup, crane, bridge

Four use repetitive activity:
gym, dance, soldier, crane  / /  snake, bath, soup, bridge

Four end in the letter 'e':
snake, dance, crane, bridge  / /  bath, gym, soldier, soup


B:

## Replace 'crane' by 'ship'.

Four are often associated with water:
bath, soup, ship, bridge  / /  snake, gym, dance, soldier

Four begin with the letter 's':
snake, soldier, soup, ship  / /  bath, gym, dance, bridge

Four provide their own energy (sometimes):
snake, soldier, ship, bridge  / /  bath, gym, dance, soup


## The Fixed Point

Alternatives are not random. Whenever we set out to generate
alternatives there is always a 'fixed point' at the back of our mind.
It is this 'fixed point' that connects up the alternatives.

## What is an alternative to a 'toothbrush'?

If the fixed point is 'cleaning teeth' then alternatives might include: a rag; chewing hard materials; some paste we smear on the teeth and leave overnight, etc.

If the fixed point is 'applying toothpaste to the teeth' then the alternatives might include: foam; finger; a stick; a lozenge, etc.

# EXERCISE 10

Suggest some alternatives to 'prison'. Be clear as to what your 'fixed point' is. Spell this out. Generate alternatives for that fixed point.

Now change the fixed point and generate alternatives for the new fixed point.

Do this as often as you can.

---

Do not turn to the next page until you have attempted this exercise

## *Exercise 10: Suggested Answers*

## The first fixed point might be 'deterrence'.

*Alternatives*:
fines
painful punishment shown on TV
publicity on convicted criminals (you cannot get away with it)
tattooing
family fines
peer-group punishment

## The second fixed point might be 'removing from society'.

*Alternatives*:
army service
work camps
house arrest
electronic bracelets (plus house confinement)

## A third fixed point might be 'restitution'.

*Alternatives*:
fines
community service
earn way out by paying victim through earnings

## A fourth fixed point might be 'retribution'.

*Alternatives*:
chopping off hands
confiscation of property
stocks
humiliation by publishing picture in newspaper
It should never be suggested that the fun of finding alternatives
should become such a habit that we refuse to do the obvious but
must always seek some other way. That would not be sensible

behaviour. In the matter of 'interest', however, the obvious is always rather dull. So in the exploration of a subject we may acknowledge the logical, sensible and obvious path, but then seek out alternatives. Most people can easily decide whether they are telling a joke or attempting to tell the truth. In exactly the same way it is possible to decide whether you are exploring a subject for the sake of interest or for the sake of practical action. It should also be said that occasionally the unusual alternative turns out to have a high practical value.

How many alternatives should you generate? There is no rule. Sometimes one is enough. At other times it is more interesting to generate several. Sometimes one alternative is so interesting that you want to pursue that alternative rather than generate other ones. There is no need to pursue each alternative in pedantic detail. Pursue only the more 'interesting ones'. That is to say the ones that are more unusual; offer more benefits; seem to be most logical.

Because fantasy is unbounded, fantasy alternatives have very little value. If anything goes so also does interest.

# EXERCISE 11

When car seat-belts were first made compulsory in the UK it seemed that car accidents decreased but at the same time motor vehicle accidents involving pedestrians actually increased. What alternative explanations can you think of?

---

Do not turn to the next page until you have attempted this exercise

## *Exercise 11: Suggested Answers*

1. If people started driving without attaching their seat-belts and then struggled to attach the belt while driving, they might more easily hit a pedestrian while attaching the belt.

2. The belt gave drivers an added sense of security, so they actually drove faster and hit more pedestrians.

3. With the belt in place it is more difficult to turn around in the driving seat, so a driver might rely more on the rear-view mirror while reversing. This poor vision might result in more pedestrian accidents.

4. Statistics were being kept more carefully in order to see the effect of the seat-belts. These more careful statistics revealed more pedestrian accidents.

5. With people not yet used to seat-belts there might have been some restriction of movement in emergency situations.

## **Formal and Informal**

The search for alternatives may be formal: 'Let's see how many alternative explanations there might be': 'That is one point of view; let's see if there could be another one'; 'That is one way of doing it – we might be able to find a better one.'

More often the search for alternatives is informal. In any situation you get into the habit of seeking out alternatives. At worst you find no alternatives so you have wasted a small amount of thinking time. You may find alternatives but none of them are better than the obvious approach. You are at least better off for having justified the current approach. You generate several reasonable alternatives. Your mind is now enriched by these possibilities. Even if they are not of use at the moment they will be of use in many future situations.

# CONCEPTS

It is unlikely that the human brain could ever have been designed by an engineer. Almost all the excellences of the human brain arise from its engineering defects. Engineers seek precision. It is the blurry nature of the human brain that is so powerful and gives rise to concepts. Imagine a camera that could only take blurry pictures. We would send it back to the engineering department with instructions to make it more precise. Biological organization is very different. The blurriness is a great advantage.

Without concepts we are stuck in detail. We might have images of several different cups. Each image might be exact but there would be no collective linking. The concept of a cup is a blurry image of something which has the nature and the function of any cup. Because it is blurry it is not any particular cup but 'cupness' in general.

Extracting concepts is one of the key operations in 'interest'. We can take a concept from a situation and then play around with that concept. We can discuss the concept itself or go on to other examples of the same concept. A particular chair might be limited and boring but the concept of 'chair' or 'sitting' could open up new avenues of thinking. Why do some cultures prefer to sit on the ground or on cushions? Perhaps because they were nomads and did not want to have to carry furniture with them. Perhaps the lack of rain made it possible to use the ground, whereas in a rainy country the mud on the ground would have ruled out sitting on the ground.

Interest largely consists in moving on from one idea to another. Amongst the different mechanisms of flow and movement, concept extraction is one of the strongest. It is not easy. Many people find dealing with concepts awkward. There is no one right answer or one right concept. There are broad concepts and there are specific concepts. The concept of 'sitting' is different from the concept of a 'chair'. There is also the concept of 'rest' and the concept of 'being in a position to do something' (such as eating).

When dealing with concepts think of:

. . . a blurry image
. . . a general function
. . . a way of doing something
. . . a method
. . . a broad classification
. . . the underlying principle
. . . a small collection of actions or things.

What is the concept of 'insurance'? At the level of purpose the concept is 'financial compensation for loss'. At the level of function the concept is 'those exposed to a risk contribute in advance to the compensation paid to whoever has the loss'. The basic concepts are 'compensation' and 'distributed contribution'.

What is the concept of education? At one level it might be 'expensive baby-sitting'. Or, it might be 'the preparation of youngsters to contribute in society'. Or, it might be 'imparting the accumulated knowledge some people believe to be necessary'. It might even be 'a self-serving system that sets its own tests and congratulates itself on preparing youngsters to pass these tests'.

Simply extracting and spelling out possible concepts can be an interesting operation. You make the effort to find the 'essence' of the system. Prejudices can be fed into the concept.

# EXERCISE 12

Link up or connect up the following pairs of randomly selected words. There may need to be several steps. Do not use stories which include both words. Seek to extract concepts and to work with these.

Example: link up 'chair' with 'gun'.
A chair allows the body to rest. So the chair supplements the natural resting features of the body. This supplementing of our natural abilities is also to be found in a gun, which amplifies our aggressive and hunting tendencies. Instead of having to run after the prey we send a bullet instead.

Link up:

teacher – wheel

headache – lake

camera – judge

cartoon – lobster

---

Do not turn the page until you have attempted this exercise

---

66

## *Exercise 12: Suggested Answers*

The purpose of a teacher is to take you forward into the subject. The teacher enables or facilitates your progress. Energy without a teacher may not get you very far. Usually the teacher makes use of existing paths or roads.

A wheel is also a method of facilitating progress. A wheel is a device to reduce friction to enable you to move forward faster. Wheels also work better on existing roads.

The problem with a headache is that it is 'there'. You are very aware of it. The headache is not progressing or getting you anywhere – it just sits there.

A lake is a body of water which is just 'there'. Unlike a river, which is going somewhere, the lake just 'is'. The lake seems very permanent and anyone with a headache has the feeling that the headache is also permanent – even if you know it is not.

The judge in a court is there to note, observe and monitor what is going on. The judge is neutral and impartial and records things as they are.

A camera is passive and neutral and designed to record matters. A camera achieves the best effect when used just at the right moment. In the same way a judge may need to intervene at the right moment.

A lobster is delicious and highly enjoyable to eat. But lobsters only get that way because they have claws which allow them to eat.

Some cartoons are also enjoyable because there is a streak of aggressive attack in them – they have 'bite'.

Concepts are the basis of so-called 'abstract' thinking. We free ourselves from the limitations of detail in order to work with the concepts we have extracted or 'abstracted'. The physical details of a game might consist of hitting a ball or catching a ball. There are mechanical items like golf clubs, tennis-rackets and baseball bats. The concept of the game is how you score, what you are trying to do and how you win. Then there are strategy concepts as to how you behave within the rules of the game in order to beat an opponent. The attraction of golf to some people is that it is a competitive sport and yet you are really playing against yourself at any moment.

With regard to the concept of a game this concept is visible to everyone. Everyone who knows the game knows what the game is about. In general, however, concepts are personal and subjective. They depend on how you want to look at something and what you want to put together as a concept. What is the concept of a 'pet'? It is easy enough to describe a canary, a dog or a cat that is loved and looked after. But the more complex concepts of 'companionship', 'being alive', 'returned affection' are all very subjective.

# EXERCISE 13

As in the preceding exercise you are being asked to make a concept link or a concept bridge between some randomly selected words. This time, however, you are asked to make bridges from one 'starting' word to four other randomly obtained words. The bridges should be as different as possible. Do not simply use a broad type of bridge which could do for all the words.

Starting word: fork

Bridges to: cow, running track, mosquito, spaghetti.

---

Do not turn to the next page until you have attempted this exercise

## *Exercise 13: Suggested Answers*

fork – cow

The function of the fork is to transfer food from a plate to our mouths. The function of a cow is to transfer the solar energy of the sun stored as food in grass through photosynthesis to our table as milk, cheese, meat, etc. The cow is a transfer device as well.

fork – running track

The fork has several parallel tines, which is why it works. The running track has several parallel lanes in order to make it more effective for shorter races.
(This is very much a descriptive concept.)

fork – mosquito

The mosquito appears to have a 'stabbing' action to get its food. A fork also functions directly through its 'stabbing' action, which is different from a spoon or chopsticks, which have lifting actions.

fork – spaghetti

A table laid out with cutlery carries the knives and forks which are the functional part of the setting. The role of spaghetti is to carry the taste of the sauce, which is the functional part of the dish. Spaghetti without sauce is as useful as a dining-table without cutlery.

# Concept Differences

Sometimes it is 'interesting' to focus on concept differences and even opposites. We can seek to contrast concepts or to show concept shifts. As usual, things which appear to be similar can be shown to be very different. And things which appear very different can, sometimes, be shown to be very similar. These give the surprises and insights that make things more interesting.

Parrots live a very long time. Should we have liquidized parrots every morning for breakfast? This bizarre suggestion opens up several concepts. There are the two competing dietary concepts. The first concept is to avoid all those things which might be harmful such as high-cholesterol food, fats, etc. Eat only fish and vegetables. The second concept holds that there are certain 'good things' and if you eat enough of these then it does not much matter what else you eat. It seems that the French have a much lower rate of heart attack than the British. Yet the French are busy eating croissants, butter, etc. They also drink wine. It seems that alcohol itself in moderation is a good thing. In addition there are factors in red wine which are also very good. Walnut oil is now a favourite 'good thing'. Flavenoids in tea are supposed to reduce the incidence of strokes. So the British should be better off in that area.

When we look for differences there has to be some point of similarity. To say that a hamburger is different from a skyscraper is not particularly interesting. But to say that both are examples of the export of American culture makes a contrast more interesting. The interesting contrast is that the skyscraper depends on mechanical efficiency (construction, steel frames, lifts, etc.) whereas the hamburger depends on functional efficiency (brand image, marketing, standardization, etc.).

# EXERCISE 14

Which food, fruit, animal and building would you choose to describe the following people?

Napoleon

Lenin

Madonna

Bill Clinton

Margaret Thatcher

For each person make your choices. These choices would be based on some 'concept' expression.

---

Do not turn to the next page until you have attempted this exercise

## *Exercise 14: Suggested Answers*

Napoleon

food: bouillabaisse; complex and full of interacting qualities
fruit: grape; the basis of the glory of wine
animal: swordfish; focused, well equipped and aggressive
building: Sydney harbour bridge; bold and very practical


Lenin

food: bread; a strong sense of the basics
fruit: water melon; large in ambition, weak in structure
animal: a rat; clever, dangerous and a survivor
building: the Eiffel tower; ambitious


The above are by way of example. You can apply your own subjective thinking to the other people in the exercise. Compare your choices with those of your friends.


## Concept Level

It is the 'effort' to find concepts and to think at the concept level that is important. Interest is made up of a number of efforts:

. . . to open up possibilities
. . . to look for alternatives
. . . to extract concepts.

# RUN FORWARD IN THE MIND

Imagine you are 'fast-forwarding' on a video recorder. In your mind you run something forward from a starting-point or scenario. What do you see happening? I could use the word 'projection' but it does not fully cover the process. You visualize and watch what you visualize. It is not on an abstract level but on a concrete 'picture' level. You watch the scene unfold. And then you talk about it. That is another ingredient in the process of 'interest'.

# EXERCISE 15

Imagine that everyone's left leg was six inches shorter than the right leg. Of course, we could compensate by having a built-up shoe on the shorter side. The exercise, however, is not about compensation but about visualizing everyday activity if this bizarre change were in place. Visualize different aspects of behaviour.

Note down what you see when running this scenario 'forward' in your mind.

---

Do not turn to the next page until you have attempted this exercise

78

## Exercise 15: Suggested Answers

1. People would tend to walk on the edge of the pavement (sidewalk) with the longer foot walking in the gutter. Perhaps pavements could be designed with a ridge down the middle. This would mean that people would walk in predetermined directions.

2. Sports such as soccer would be difficult. Golfers would carry a little step to even things up.

3. Difficulty with accelerator and brake pedals in a car. Great difficulty with bicycle pedals since just making one pedal arm longer would not work.

4. New dances with much more body movement. Dancing face to face would be difficult because the partners would sway in opposite directions.

5. Stairs and ladders might need to be redesigned though this would not be essential.

6. Walking on the side of hills or slopes would be much easier.

7. People might develop a sort of hopping gait.

8. Boxers would have a more tricky target.

9. Swimmers might tend to swim round in a circle if one leg gave more propulsion than the other.

10. Scooters would be easier to use and much in demand (or single roller skates).

The purpose of running something forward is to examine consequences. What would happen if . . . ? Once there is a skill in running things forward in the mind then it becomes possible to use speculation and provocation in order to enrich the field of interest.

There is also a more serious side to examining the possible consequences of suggestions and alternatives.

# EXERCISE 16

In China there is a 'one-child' policy in an attempt to restrict population growth. But families often want at least one son. This leads to difficulties. Suppose there was a rule that every family could have as many children as they like but would have to stop having children as soon as the first boy was born.

Run this suggestion forward in your mind and see what you find. Note down your thoughts.

---

Do not turn to the next page until you have attempted this exercise

## *Exercise 16: Suggested Answers*

At first sight it would seem that there would be many more girls. Some families might have four girls before having a boy. Some families might even have seven girls and never have a boy. But no family could have more than one boy.

Actually the population would be evenly balanced. Since no baby is actually being killed the distribution of boy/girl births would remain exactly the same. So the number of boy and girl children would be equal (actually a slight difference depending on many factors such as water hardness). It seems counter-intuitive but you can work it out with a diagram.

Sometimes something which seems attractive turns out not to be so when we run it forward and look at all the possible consequences. Politicians have to do this all the time in order to see what votes a proposition might gain or lose. At other times, something which seems unattractive at first turns out to have some merits after all.

Since all proposed actions are going to take place in the future and since we can only imagine the future, the skill of running things forward in the mind is important.

# EXERCISE 17

There is a suggestion that prisoners who have been in prison a long time should be given a pension on release. Run the possible reactions and consequences forward in your mind.

---

Do not turn to the next page until you have attempted this exercise

## *Exercise 17: Suggested Answers*

1. Public horror and media outrage at the idea that criminals were actually being rewarded.

2. Outrage at the idea that going to prison was a good way to get a pension. Comparisons with people who had worked hard and honestly for many years to get a pension.

3. Outrage at the cost of the scheme.

4. Prisoners would have something to live on and would not have to fall back on crime.

5. Prisoners would now have 'something to lose' if they went back to crime and might prefer not to.

6. The cost of the pension would be very much less than the cost of convicting that prisoner if he or she reverted to crime, and then keeping the prisoner in prison. In the USA it would be cheaper to send a prisoner to Harvard University than to keep that prisoner in prison.

7. People might choose to commit certain types of crime which usually received sentences just long enough to earn the pension.

## Joint Exploration

The process of 'running something forward' in your mind can be an individual exercise or a joint one. You can invite someone else to join you in the exploration. One party or the other might suggest an aspect of the situation and invite the other to visualize it. For example, in the exercise involving one leg being shorter than the other leg the following remarks might have been made:

'Let's see what might happen in sport . . .'

'What about day-to-day living; moving about the house; walking down the street . . .'

'How would this affect leisure activities?'

'What would be the effect on children?'

'Can you think of any situation where it might be an advantage?'

'How would it affect going up stairs?'

It is this interaction and the generation of different views which creates the interest.

It is possible to deal with the consequences in a broad sense or in a very detailed sense.

'How do you think most people would react to the idea of giving pensions to discharged prisoners?'

'Imagine a sixty-five-year-old man who has worked hard all his life to get a small pension. How would that person react to the idea that a prisoner discharged after ten years in prison gets an equal pension?'

# EXERCISE 18

Today young women in many countries seem much more willing to take the initiative in matters of dating, courting and marrying. If this becomes a strong trend to the extent that it becomes customary for women to propose marriage, what do you see happening?

Run this forward not only with regard to ultimate consequences but also with regard to day-to-day behaviour.

---

Do not turn to the next page until you have attempted this exercise

## *Exercise 18: Suggested Answers*

1. A possible shift from 'looks' to 'personality'. Instead of a young woman having to look wonderful in order to attract attention, that person can now use her personality directly.

2. Shy men will find they are more appreciated than they had ever been before.

3. Men will become very lazy and expect women to do all the pursuing.

4. 'Suitable' young men will be faced with the problem of how to turn people on without offending them.

5. Young men might become spoiled and callous.

6. Girls will be much less worried about breaking off an unsuitable relationship because it is within their control to start a new one.

7. Men will have to pay much more attention to what women like.

8. Women will have more influence on culture. If women show they are not impressed by macho strutting then this will disappear.

9. Timid girls will have a very hard time.

10. Some women may become very aggressive and competitive with other women.

Some people have 'eidetic' memories. They can visualize a whole airline schedule and then 'read off' the information they need. It is not possible to develop such a memory through effort or practice. But practice does make it possible to 'run things forward in our minds' more effectively. It is the intention to do so and the pause to try that is important. It will not just happen if you never try. If you try you will get better and better at it.

# CONNECT AND LINK UP

The process of connecting up and linking up different matters is basic to the process of 'interest'.

There are two key types of connection.

1. How do you link up something that is being said to your own experience, knowledge and feelings?

2. How do you link up one thing with another in order to keep going forward along an alley of interest?

Gossip works well because what is said immediately links up with people you know directly, or indirectly as celebrities. As the gossip accumulates there is more to know and more to link up with.

Sports fans have interesting conversations because they already know so much about players, games, league-table positions, that new information has much to link up with. Special-interest groups work in the same way.

In general terms, something is interesting if it can be linked back to the individuals taking part in the discussion or to human behaviour in general (and hence to individuals in an indirect way). This very important aspect of 'relevance' will be discussed in a later section of this book. It is fundamental to the process of interest. Why is this of interest to me?

A skilled politician on television will always answer the question he or she wants to answer. Whatever question the interviewer puts forward, the politicians, through a series of clever linkages, will bring it back to the answer he or she wants to give.

In the same way, 'connecting up' allows us to bring in thoughts, feelings, experience and special knowledge. We find ways of linking these in to the ongoing discussion.

'That reminds me of the time when . . .'

'Talking about bridges, did you know that London bridge . . . ?'

'Coming back to your point about restaurants, have you ever . . . ?'

'I want to tell you another story about poodles . . .'

## Associations and Triggers

A 'trigger' is a very loose form of connection. Some word or concept simply triggers your thoughts about a subject. Unless what you have to contribute is particularly interesting in itself, which it might be, triggers can actually diminish interest through disrupting the flow of a conversation: if, for example, in an interesting conversation about walruses someone is triggered to wonder why 'walrus moustaches have become less fashionable'. There is a fine balance between the lightness and variety of conversation and continual disruption.

Association is also a relatively weak form of connection. The association might be very personal and therefore not of interest to others. It therefore appears as a disjunction in the conversation. If the matter introduced in this way is itself of interest then the association has a value.

# EXERCISE 19

Below, on the left-hand side, there is a list of ten random words. On the right-hand side there is a list of ten associations. Each of the associations arises from one of the words in the first list. Try to match them up so each association is matched with one of the words in the first list. An association can only be matched with one word.

| | |
|---|---|
| cigarette | pain |
| doctor | night |
| garage | delay |
| rocket | holes |
| computer | match |
| law | hospital |
| pin | confusion |
| airport | dark |
| bat | control |
| cheese | storage |

---

Do not turn to the next page until you have attempted this exercise

---

## *Exercise 19: Suggested Answers*

This very easy exercise is, of course, totally subjective. There is no one right answer because everyone can have different associations. One set of matchings is shown below:

| | |
|---|---|
| cigarette | match |
| doctor | hospital |
| garage | dark |
| rocket | control |
| computer | storage |
| law | delay |
| pin | pain |
| airport | confusion |
| bat | night |
| cheese | holes |

Associations may be immediate and obvious or personal and remote. What seems a direct association to one person may seem a random connection to another.

## Functional Links

Suppose you were asked to link up the words: wine, typewriter, newspaper and shampoo.

'I went shopping in the morning and bought some wine, some paper for my typewriter, shampoo and a newspaper.'

'As I was walking down the high street I noticed some wine at a sale price. In the next shop there were typewriters. On the corner was a man selling newspapers. Then I remembered I had to buy some shampoo.'

Those sorts of connection are weak and boring.

Functional links examine concepts, uses, values, similarities, differences and other aspects instead of just stringing together the items in a story-line.

Skill in establishing strong functional links adds to interest because the flow from one idea to another now has a basis. The mind is now engaged, which it is not in a simple story-line connection.

CONCEPTS: This relates back to 'concept extraction'. What concepts do we find here?

USES: What is the purpose or function? Can a case be made for a similarity of purpose?

VALUES: Why is this of value? Does the other matter offer the same value?

SIMILARITY: In what way is this similar? Do they possess something in common?

DIFFERENCE: Is the difference sharp enough to be an 'opposite' or a 'contrast'? Something may be similar in some respects but very different in others.

# EXERCISE 20

In any way you like, link up each of the following random words with the activity of 'buying a car'. Seek to make the connections as different as possible.

umbrella

telephone

butterfly

volcano

star

---

Do not turn to the next page until you have attempted this exercise

---

## Exercise 20: Suggested Answers

umbrella / rain / wet roads / skidding / what are the road-holding characteristics of this car / can I easily handle it?

telephone / communication / what do I really need the car for? / commuting to work? / leisure?

butterfly / more beauty than functionality / am I being over-impressed by the appearance of the car?

volcano / unexpected eruptions and disasters / what is the track record of these cars for breakdowns / what is the cost of repairs and spare parts?

star / the focus of attention / do I want a 'show-off' car or a quiet one? / star cars might be more easily stolen.

## Keep Going

The purpose of connecting things up is to 'keep going'. Outside special-interest areas there are a few subjects which are sustainable entirely on their own. Skill in linking things up means that other aspects or other subjects can be brought in. The important thing is that it should be done smoothly. Otherwise there is the artificiality of seeming to have a 'shopping-list' of things to talk about and going down the list item by item.

As usual, it is the activity of the mind around a subject that makes it interesting for both the speaker and the listener. Connections are doors that are opened so both parties can proceed through that door into another room.

If you become skilled at connecting things up then no starting-point is ever too boring because you can move on to aspects or connections that are interesting.

'Keeping going' does not imply speed or a race. There is no hurry. You travel along the road of interest at leisure. You pause and look around. You dawdle and pick flowers. You stop to talk to other people. It should never be a rush to get from A to B as fast as possible.

# EXERCISE 21

A cruise ship is scheduled to call at different ports. The sequence of ports is chosen to make the journey as interesting as possible. Imagine that each of the six randomly chosen words is a 'port of call'. Plan the movement from one word to another so that in the end all words have been 'visited'. The journey between each word must be justified by a strong connection.

sport

ice

lipstick

laser

salt

saw

---

Do not turn to the next page until you have attempted this exercise

---

## Exercise 21: Suggested Answers

'salt' to 'lipstick'

Too much salt is bad. Too little salt is bland. Perhaps it is the same with cosmetics. There is the need for just the right amount.

'lipstick' to 'sport'

People find each other attractive. Why should flirtation not be a sort of sport? It does not have to be taken seriously or lead on to anything else. Some cultures can handle this but others do not seem able to.

'sport' to 'laser'

Could we not use lasers as a basis for sport? Instead of guns we could use lasers. There was a game for youngsters in which they shot at each other with lasers. Perhaps there could be a non-aggressive type of sport with lasers. Shooting at moving targets and a radio signal back if your laser hit the target.

'laser' to 'ice'

Using lasers for ice sculpture. You melt and shape the ice. Then you might make a quick mould with plastic and you have a real permanent sculpture.

'ice' to 'saw'

Could a very rapid oscillation between heat and cold be used to 'cut' or crack certain materials like rock – instead of using a mechanical drill?

Connections can bring in special knowledge, speculation, questions, possibilities and all the other aspects of the interest process.

# PROVOCATION

Provocation is fun.

Provocation is an essential part of creative thinking.

What is the definition of a provocation?

'There may not be a reason for saying something until after it has been said.'

That is rather different from ordinary thinking where there should be a reason for saying something before that thing is said. In provocation the thoughts set off by the provocation are the justification for the provocation in the first place.

The human brain works as a self-organizing information system. This means that asymmetric patterns are formed. There is a mathematical need for provocation in order to cut across the patterns to open up new ones (creativity). Those interested in these aspects of deliberate and formal creativity (lateral thinking) should read my book *Serious Creativity* (HarperCollins).

Provocation is such an essential part of thinking that many years ago I invented a word to signal that a provocation was being made. That word is 'po'. 'Po cars have square wheels' is signalled as a provocation. It is not intended to be a direct practical suggestion. That provocation actually leads to the concept of 'intelligent suspension'.

Provocation overlaps with speculation but goes further. A hypothesis should have a 'reasonable' basis. A speculation does not need that reasonable basis but the speculation should not be outrageous or contrary to normal experience. A provocation can be outrageous and contrary to normal experience. That is its very function. To jump the mind out of its usual tracks. Because the provocation is deliberately signalled as a provocation (by the word 'po') the provocation can be as bold and provocative as you like.

The whole point about a provocation is that it does have to be provocative. There is no point at all in putting forward a weak provocation.

There are in fact formal ways of creating provocations (described in the book *Serious Creativity*) but there is no need to go into such detail here. It is enough to emphasize that provocations should be bold and contrary to normal experience.

## EXERCISE 22

Below is a list of ten provocations. Select the five which you consider to be the boldest. Then set up three more bold provocations of your own in the same subject area.

Po criminals should compensate their victims.

Po criminals are paid to commit crime.

Po there should be more police on foot.

Po street gangs should be responsible for order in their area.

Po any crime committed on Monday gets double the sentence.

Po there should be night classes to make better criminals.

Po sentencing should be standardized and known to all.

Po the sentence doubles for each new conviction.

Po victims choose the punishment for their attackers.

Po thieves have their hands chopped off.

When you have completed your selection, add three of your own.

---

Do not turn to the next page until you have attempted this exercise

## *Exercise 22: Suggested Answers*

The choice is obviously subjective. I have listed below the ones I consider the most provocative. This does not necessarily mean they will lead to the best ideas.

*Most provocative*

Po criminals are paid to commit crime.
Po street gangs should be responsible for order in their area.
Po any crime committed on Monday gets double the sentence.
Po there should be night classes to make better criminals.
Po victims choose the punishment for their attackers.

*Less provocative*

Po criminals should compensate their victims.
Po there should be more police on foot.
Po sentencing should be standardized and known to all.
Po the sentence doubles for each new conviction.
Po thieves have their hands chopped off.

All these are somewhat reasonable suggestions. In some cultures thieves do have their hands chopped off.

## Use of Provocations

When you have a provocation you 'run it forward' in your mind. You can 'extract the concept'. You can 'explore possibilities'. You can make 'connections'. You can examine for 'benefits and values'. Most of these processes have already been considered. They apply equally to provocations as to any other situation.

The provocation provides an unusual starting-point from which we 'move' forward with the process known as 'movement'.

'Movement' is quite different from 'judgement'. With judgement we are concerned with whether someone is right or wrong, fits or does not fit our experience. With 'movement' we are only concerned with moving forwards to a new idea. Movement is an active mental process, not just the suspension of judgement.

At the end we do want to come back to an idea that has value, is practical or at least is 'interesting'.

In the practical use of lateral thinking we do intend to end up with an idea which is practical and valuable. Where provocation is being used to stimulate interest it is enough that new and interesting ideas are produced. These can lead to insights and new considerations.

For example, the provocation: 'Po criminals should attend night classes to make them better criminals', could lead to the idea of spelling out very clearly the behaviour that takes criminals into another class of crime. The use of guns or knives as a threat might make the crime much worse. So would the presence of an accomplice. In practice, such considerations are often taken into account, but they need to be widely known by potential criminals.

# EXERCISE 23

Take each of the provocations given below and try to 'move forward' from them.

Look at what might happen.

See who benefits.

Observe what new concepts might emerge.

1. Po there is no television on Thursdays.
2. Po women are all taller than men.

---

Do not turn to the next page until you have attempted this exercise

## *Exercise 23: Suggested Answers*

1. Juvenile crime might increase on Thursdays. Other forms of entertainment might focus especially on Thursdays. People would eat out or make social arrangements for Thursdays. Human conversation might get a chance. This break in the television-watching habit might lead to a decline in viewing. Revenue would drop for television stations. Newspapers would get increased sales on Friday mornings. Television personnel would get a day of rest. On Thursdays the TV set might be used for access to the Internet.

2. Men would wear tall hats like tops hats, stove-pipe hats and bearskins. Men would wear elevated shoes. Men might want to be mothered and dominated. Cocktail parties would disappear, as all socializing would be done sitting down. Thinness would no longer be fashionable. Robust women would be in fashion. Men might more easily accept women in business and in politics. Women might come to regard men as dispensable studs.

The unusual starting-point provided by provocations makes for interesting speculation. Instead of just describing personal experiences or giving information about a situation, there is now the fun of exploration. What is most interesting is the exploration of different ideas. It is more interesting to suppose that men would accept women more easily in business than to suppose that men would wear tall hats.

As soon as you get a new or interesting idea arising from the provocation you can concentrate on that idea and forget about the provocation. For example, if the concept is 'that physical appearance' makes women seem more powerful, then a practical suggestion would be for women to wear tall hats at all times at work. What effect would that have? A whole area of exploration now opens up.

From the movement that arises from a provocation we can select themes, avenues and alleys of exploration. There is no obligation to explore all of them if the main purpose of our discussion is 'interest'.

## Interest Sensitivity

The 'drivers' of interest include: emotions, feelings, surprises, fascination, relevance, personal relevance, etc. These will all be considered in later sections. For the moment I want to focus on sensitivity to interest. Some photographic films are much more sensitive to light than others: i.s.o. 400 is much more sensitive than i.s.o. 100. In the same way we can develop a sensitivity to interest.

. . . this leads to many things

. . . this is different from the normal

. . . this offers benefits and values

. . . this suggests a new way of looking at things

. . . this has direct relevance to human behaviour

. . . this would solve a particular problem

. . . this changes the focus

# EXERCISE 24

Po wages are not paid uniformly. Every fourth week the wage is doubled. Other weeks are reduced to give the same overall pay.

People might borrow more. People might live on the basic wage and use the extra amount for saving or luxury items. There might arise a distinction between 'living' wage and 'capital' wage. There might be more careful budgeting. The fourth week 'bonus' might be regarded as a bonus. This bonus might also be increased depending on the profitability of the company. The introduction of non-uniform wages might lead on to a genuine bonus element in the pay.

From these 'movement' points select out the one that you feel to be most interesting. Explain why.

---

Do not turn to the next page until you have attempted this exercise

---

## *Exercise 24: Suggested Answers*

I feel the most interesting point is the possibility of people coming to look at money in two different ways: current-expenses money and 'capital' money. The fourth-week extra wage might come to be seen as 'capital'. This could have a powerful effect on investment attitudes and savings. This in turn would have a powerful effect on the economy. There is some evidence that this might happen, from Japan, where the custom is a basic wage with large bonuses twice a year. These tend to be used for investment.

Once the skills of provocation and movement have been developed, they become a powerful way of injecting interest into any discussion. Discussions become boring when they proceed along the routine lines with everyone offering routine information and routine opinions. Provocation is a way of escaping from this boredom. The brain finds it difficult to think afresh just because it is told to do so. The use of provocation goes beyond the mere intention to have new ideas. Provocations actually force the mind to have new thoughts.

## **ATTENTION-DIRECTING**

How would we manage if we were never allowed to ask a question?

'What time is it?'

'What is your name?'

'How much does this cost?'

'Where is the bathroom?'

'Who told you that?'

At first it might seem that life would be very awkward if we were never allowed to ask questions. In fact it would make very little difference.

'Direct your attention to the time.'

'Direct attention to your name.'

'Tell me the cost of this.'

'Tell me where the bathroom is.'

'Direct your attention to the origin of that.'

A question is just a very simple way of asking someone to direct his or her attention to some particular matter. Direct your attention and then tell me what you find or see.

Most thinking is a matter of directing attention.

Direct attention to the consequences of this.

Direct attention to the benefits / dangers.

Direct attention to the alternatives.

Direct attention to other people's views.

The very successful CORT Thinking Programme, which is now being used throughout the world for the direct teaching of thinking as a skill in schools, makes use of 'attention-directing tools'. The DATT programme for business does the same.

Imagine a house. You can direct your attention to the facade as a whole; to the windows; to the entrance. In your imagination you enter the house and can now direct your attention to each room in turn.

You can instruct an explorer to look north and to note down what he or she sees. Then east, then south and then west. Frames for directing attention are much in use.

In the process of 'interest', the directing of attention is very important. You pick on something that has been said and encourage others to direct their attention to that matter. Not only do you suggest directing attention to the matter but you may also suggest how you direct attention.

In discussing traffic congestion in cities someone may mention the need for more taxis. You choose to focus upon that. You may then suggest a provocation: 'Po every car can choose to be a taxi.' You may then wish to add special information. In Peru every car can choose to become a taxi; you just put a card in the window saying 'taxi' and you are a taxi.

Not everything that is said is of equal interest. It may even be that the main line of conversation is rather boring. So you focus on one particular remark and use it to open up a new avenue of interest. Skill in doing that is part of the skill of interest.

# EXERCISE 25

To which point in the following passage would you like to direct your attention? Give your choice and explain why.

'People's perception of values is often very different from reality. The price of silver is usually in the range of $5–10 per ounce. The price of gold is usually in the range of $350–400. The price of platinum is in the range of $400–450. Yet in a jeweller's shop most people think that gold is probably about twice as expensive as silver and that platinum is twice as expensive as gold. Naturally, jewellers want to preserve this illusion. The jeweller would rightly claim that the price reflected the workmanship put into the object. Also, in terms of value, if you believe silver to be more valuable than it is then, for you, that is the real value. How would people react to silver if they knew it was only about one seventieth of the price of gold?'

Do not turn to the next page until you have attempted this exercise

## *Exercise 25: Suggested Answers*

Here are some possible focus points from the passage.

1. That people's perception of value may be very different from reality. What other examples come to mind?

2. Why is gold so much more expensive than silver? Is it the difficulty of getting gold? Is it the price people have been prepared to pay? Is it because it never tarnishes? Is it because it looks better?

3. If you believe something to have a high value then it has, for you. Is the illusion of value real value?

4. In a survey how many people would know that the raw cost of silver was only one seventieth of the cost of gold?

5. What is the point of view of the jeweller?

# Sensitization

A fanatical feminist listening to a conversation or a lecture is highly sensitized to any remark that could be interpreted as keeping women in a less important role than that of men. This frame of sensitization allows the person to pick up any such remark no matter how slight or unintended.

If you are coming in to land in an airplane you often fly over the airport car park. If you instruct your mind to 'pick out the yellow cars' then you suddenly find that every yellow car seems to 'pop up' from amongst the others.

The biological value of sensitization is obvious. If a lion is hunting a zebra then the lion is sensitized to notice young or weak zebras and so pick them out as prey. A zebra is sensitized to notice a lion, so if there is any sound or disturbance the zebra will be prepared to pick out the lion.

Sensitization prepares the mind to notice things. We give instructions to the mind to direct attention to one thing or to another.

There are some traditional frames of 'sensitization' which are always in mind.

. . . human behaviour
. . . men/women relationships
. . . sex
. . . money
. . . power
. . . celebrity gossip

All newspaper editors know these frames automatically and arrange their pages accordingly.

If you have special knowledge in an area then that also becomes a frame of sensitization. You listen to the conversation in order to pick up a point of possible connection so that you may introduce your special knowledge. Sometimes this does add to the interest. Sometimes it can be boring if you try to steer every conversation around to the same field of interest.

## The Pause

If you are driving along the road you do notice some things beside the road. If, however, you pause in your driving with the deliberate intention of looking around, then you will notice very much more.

It is the same with a flow of conversation. One point leads to another and the flow continues. If, however, you create a 'mental pause' then you can stop at some point in order to look around. You can elaborate around that point. You can use the point as the start of a new avenue or alley of interest.

The pause can be internal to yourself or you can suggest the pause to others: 'Let's stop for a moment at this point. Why . . . ?'

# EXERCISE 26

In the following passage indicate some possible 'pause' points.

'In the old days the Inuit people of Canada (formerly known as the Eskimo) used to spend the long dark months of winter huddled together in an igloo. That may or may not explain why they have developed a rich perceptual language. For instance there may be one word which says: "I like you very much but I would not go seal hunting with you." Someone would be "perceived" through that word. That is quite different from describing someone in conversation as "not being the sort of person with whom you would go seal hunting". Developed languages often lose the power of perception because it is believed that description is enough. Because something can be elegantly described does not mean that it can be perceived in that way.'

---

Do not turn to the next page until you have attempted this exercise

---

## *Exercise 26: Suggested Answers*

Suggested 'pauses' after the following words in the passage.

after 'Eskimo': why has the name been changed?

after 'igloo': what do they do now? How long were they in the igloos? What must it have been like at close quarters for so long?

after 'perceptual language': what does that mean?

after 'not go seal hunting with you': we can imagine the sort of people we might say that to. Entertaining people but hopelessly impractical or unreliable. Nice to be able to separate out different grades of 'like'.

after 'describing': why is perception so different from describing?

after 'developed languages': what do we mean by developed? In what way are they more developed than primitive languages?

after 'description': perhaps literature has wrecked language by putting all the emphasis on 'description' rather than 'perception'.


## **The Dance of Attention**

Aesthetics is no more than the choreography of attention. In a beautiful work of art our attention is taken on a dance: from the whole to a part; back to the whole; from one feature to another; from one emotion to another; from a relation to itself to a relation to life; and so on.

High skill in the 'interest' process also involves this dance of attention. There has to be a feeling of when to move on. When to get involved in detail and when to work with broad concepts. When to speculate on relevance and when to leave it at a suggestion level. The lively dance of interest is different from the pompous march of boredom.

## ALLEYS, AVENUES AND THEMES

Interest is much more like exploring an old town than driving along a superhighway. Interest is not a matter of getting from A to B as quickly as you can. Interest is not a matter of proving your point or ramming your opinion down other people's throats. Interest is not a matter of preaching or making political speeches. Interest is a mutual exploration of what is interesting.

Unlike the meeting of a board of directors or the meeting of a consultant with a client, there is not a fixed agenda or road map. It is not a matter of taking one road first and then another. There is no road map. It is like driving without a road map. You follow your interest. If a road seems interesting then you take it.

There are broad avenues of interest as in Paris or Buenos Aires. There are quaint alleys of interest as in Mdina (Malta) or St Paul-de-Vence (France).

As we enter any road, avenue or alley we make our choice based on two or three things. There is the starting-point. There is the general direction. There might even be a glimpse of what is promised. It is exactly the same with interest. There is the starting-point or point of departure. This may arise from the 'pauses' described in a previous section. There is a general sense of direction. There may also be some particular items which appear in that direction.

There is no bold road sign to indicate a possible avenue or alley. You need to be 'sensitized' to spot the potential beginning of an avenue or alley.

# EXERCISE 27

From the following passage pick out some possible avenues or alleys of interest. Give some indication of why you think they might be interesting. Make full notes of your thinking before returning to the main section.

'The great philosopher Aristotle was the tutor of Alexander the Great. Alexander was probably the most successful general ever. By the age of twenty-six he had conquered all the "known" world. From his starting-point in Macedonia he had taken his troops as far as India – where there are still said to be fair-haired descendants of his troops. At the age of twenty-six he died either of illness or through poison.'

---

Do not turn to the next page until you have attempted this exercise

---

## *Exercise 27: Suggested Answers*

There would be the following avenues and alleys of interest.

1. Alexander's father (Philip of Macedonia) must himself have been a remarkable man. His choice of Aristotle as a tutor possibly indicated the way the boy was brought up. This upbringing may have led to his success.

2. Perhaps Aristotle did indeed make Alexander into a powerful thinker and this was the basis of his success. This opens up the very interesting area of 'thinking' and 'doing'. Are they as separate as is usually supposed?

3. Perhaps Aristotle did not actually make Alexander a better thinker but gave Alexander supreme confidence in his decisions because they seemed to arise from a logical basis. This confidence could have been the key to his success. We can see such confidence as the basis of the success of the Normans, of Frederick of Prussia, of Napoleon, of Garibaldi, etc. For many years after Bjorn Borg won at Wimbledon, many of the top tennis players in the world were Swedish (a small country of only 8 million people and very little summer).

4. Alexander at the age of twenty-six was remarkably young to have achieved so very much. What about achievement and age? When Napoleon was finished and on his way to St Helena he was younger than John Kennedy when he became the 'young President'.

5. The career of Alexander was terminated at so young an age by illness or poison. What might he have achieved if he had lived longer? Was he only a man of action?

6. Even the most powerful people are highly vulnerable to illness or poison.

7. What was the secret of Alexander's military success? Better weapons? Better strategy? Better training? Better discipline and motivation? What are the lessons to be learned?

## Choice of Avenue or Alley

There are a number of reasons why you might seek to open up some avenue or alley of interest.

1. It is a subject area of interest in itself. For example, it may relate to some of the fundamental interest themes such as the relationship between the sexes.

2. It is a subject area that you feel would be of particular interest to those taking part in the discussion.

3. You have something particular to add to that area. This could be information, ideas, speculations, etc.

4. You feel that others might have something special to say about that area. It may be a way of drawing out that interest.

5. You want to escape from a line of thinking that has become boring.

In general, 'richness' and 'relevance' form the basis for choice. There are occasions when a single theme is fascinating in itself even if it is low on relevance or richness. That is exceptional. The key questions to ask are:

Why is this interesting to me?

Why would this be interesting to others?

It may be that the general theme is interesting. It may be that special knowledge or experience about the subject is interesting.

# EXERCISE 28

From the following passage pick out some avenues or alleys of interest. Explain why you think these particular lines of thinking would be of interest.

'It seems that having a below-normal level of zinc can cause increased aggressiveness. A zinc-rich diet is now being tried in prisons. Mostly zinc comes from yeast. If you do not drink wine or alcohol and do not have leavened bread then you may be short of zinc. Men lose some zinc every time they make love. Oysters are rich in zinc. Perhaps the solution to some of the world's problems may lie in oysters, Marmite or Vegemite (spreads based on yeast extracts).'

---

Do not turn to the next page until you have attempted this exercise

## *Exercise 28: Suggested Answers*

1. The very broad 'avenue' that diet may be responsible for behaviour. This opens up both the 'interest' of explaining certain behaviours and also the hope of modifying behaviours through dietary choice or supplements. This theme links in with the growing interest in special vitamins, minerals and other food additives. People want more control over ageing, over looks, over illness and over behaviour. Taking a pill once a day is a simple and powerful way of doing all this – if it works.

2. The avenue of 'responsibility' for behaviour. If our diet determines what we do, how responsible are we for that behaviour?

3. The suggestion that men may be more zinc-deficient than women and hence more aggressive. Also the connection with oysters, which have been traditionally seen as an aphrodisiac; but they would not work for women. The interest here is based on men/women relationships and sex.

4. The possibilities of research. Should we be measuring zinc levels in different parts of the world?

## Alleys

Avenues are broad, sweeping directions of interest. Alleys are little side turnings. We may turn off down an alley and then return to the main avenue again. An alley is never intended to be a major change of direction. An alley is a small-scale exploration. There may be just one point of interest to be explored. Alleys often have hidden entrances. They are not easily noticed. You have to be on the lookout for them.

# EXERCISE 29

In the following passage pick out three possible 'alleys' of interest. Try to avoid the broad avenues or themes.

'Among the coral reefs in Australia there are certain fish which change sex on demand. If there are not enough female fish then some males change into females. If there are not enough male fish then some females change into males. The fish of changed sex are fully functional in their new role.'

---

Do not turn to the next page until you have attempted this exercise

---

## Exercise 29: Suggested Answers

Here are three possible 'alleys' of interest.

1. How is the 'signal' passed amongst the fish? Is it a chemical in the water? Is it increasing frustration of one sex which cannot find a mate?

2. Who responds to the signal first? Is it those nearest in nature to the opposite sex?

3. How big does the imbalance have to be before the changes are triggered? Can there be overcompensation?

These are really 'alleys'.

The broad 'avenues' might have been:

1. Sex and sex change

2. Chemical and hormonal effects on gender

3. Social needs and gender behaviour.

## Themes

There is a great deal of overlap between avenues, alleys and themes. An avenue is a broad line of thought. An alley is a smaller, temporary exploration. A theme is the broadest of all and indicates a large subject area. For instance 'gender change' might be a theme. So might 'social self-adjusting systems' (in the previous exercise).

Like concepts, themes have to be extracted and defined. They are rarely laid out explicitly as 'themes'. You need to extract the theme, define it clearly and then offer it for exploration. It is probably better to be explicit about a theme rather than just decide the theme internally for yourself.

'I think this theme of gender change is interesting . . .'

'Let's look at the theme of social needs and gender distribution . . .'

'There is this theme of overspecialization. Fish can change sex but we cannot because we have become too specialized.'

# EXERCISE 30

What broad themes can you extract from the following passage?

'A man was acquitted of the crime of murder because he claimed that he had killed the victim while sleepwalking. He demonstrated that he had had a previous history of sleepwalking.

'There are a few people who genuinely have multiple personalities. There are different people organized within the same brain. What happens when one of these "people" commits a crime? Do the innocent persons have to be punished?'

Do not turn to the next page until you have attempted this exercise

## *Exercise 30: Suggested Answers*

There could be the following themes.

1. The key concept of 'responsibility' in committing a crime. In most countries alcohol is no longer an excuse. Even if the person did not really know what he or she was doing because of alcohol, that is no longer an excuse because the person freely drank the alcohol and must take responsibility for all the consequences. But a person is not responsible for sleepwalking.

2. The key theme of the 'practicality' of law. It might seem that sleepwalking was an alibi that could very frequently be used – and could also be built up to in advance. What happens if it became a general reason? The practicality of the law in dealing with multiple personalities. Is there a fair way of dealing with this? How much can law be about practicality as well as principle?

# CLARIFY, LIST AND SUMMARIZE

There are some people who have the ability to make something that is very simple appear very complex. Such people are unconscious experts at confusing both themselves and others. Not only can they not see the wood for the trees, but they cannot even see the trees because they are looking only at the leaves.

There are other people who have the marvellous ability to take complex matters and to make them appear quite simple. Such people can see to the heart of the matter. Such people can discard what is detail and what is irrelevant.

Not surprisingly, simplicity horrifies those people who cannot be simple. Those who do not have the ability to see through to the heart of the matter genuinely believe that it is the complexity of the detail which really matters. So they dismiss as 'simplistic' anything which does not follow the complexity of detail. Unfortunately many academics and critics fall into this category. They hate simplicity because there is then very little to write about. Also there is the ultimate dilemma. Is this person writing so simply because he or she really understands the subject, or is the person writing simply because he or she has only a superficial view of the subject? It takes an honest brain to make the distinction.

Three Nobel prizewinners wrote forewords to my book *I am Right – You are Wrong*. One of them remarked that in order to express something simply you had to really know your subject. Whenever I talk to top-level mathematicians and physicists they can understand the full implications of expressing something simply. Too many philosophers, psychologists and journalists cannot. Such people are bogged down with wordplay and cannot see beyond the words.

Being able to clarify something and to communicate it in a simple way is part of the interest process. While 'richness' is an important part of interest, 'confusion' is not. People who are confused may seem to be having an interesting time because there is a lot of to-and-fro discussion. But the overall feeling is one of confusion and waste of time. The after-taste is bad.

Analogies and metaphors are powerful ways of expressing complex relationships. Analogies can never 'prove' anything but they can show the possibility of a relationship. That possibility now has to be considered.

We usually think that if something is good then, surely, more of it is better. You might gave many examples of where and why this is not the case. Too much chocolate cake may make children ill. Too many marriages may make a person careless. A simple analogy can clarify the whole process.

There is the salt curve. No salt is bad. Some salt is good. Too much salt is bad. In economics, Arthur Laffer set out to show that too much taxation actually reduced the tax take because people made more strenuous efforts to avoid paying tax.

# EXERCISE 31

How would you describe the following situation with a simple analogy?

'A government gradually increases taxes. There is more and more complaint. One day there is a revolution and people refuse to pay their taxes.'

---

Do not turn to the next page until you have attempted this exercise

## *Exercise 31: Suggested Answers*

1. There is the traditional analogy: 'the straw that breaks the camel's back'. The load can be made heavier and heavier but at some point the final 'straw' makes the load too heavy.

2. You are pushing against an empty glass. You push and you push and suddenly the glass falls over.

3. The effect is sometimes known as 'the threshold effect'. Nothing happens until rising water reaches the height of the threshold and then your house floods.

4. A rowing-boat takes on more and more water from the choppy seas. Suddenly the boat sinks.

## Complex Situations

Systems, relationships and abstract matters can be complex. Often it is easier to show them pictorially with diagrams. This helps where it is possible. At other times we may need to simplify something in order to understand it. We may need to bring it down to its essence.

# EXERCISE 32

Seek to simplify the following passage in order to present its essence.

'Society depends upon good judgement. We need to judge whether something is true, whether it would work, whether it fits our values and objectives, and so on. Critical thinking is the key method we have for exercising this judgement. The word "critical" comes from the Greek word for judge, which is *kritikos*. It would be very difficult for society to work if we did not use critical thinking. But judgement is not enough. There is the need for the generative, productive, constructive and creative side of thinking. How do things happen? How do things get done? Selection and judgement is fine – but there has to be something to judge. The traditions of thinking have been dominated by critical thinking because the doers are out there producing and the only people directly interested in thinking have been the critics. That is why thinking has been dangerously dominated by the notion that critical thinking is enough. That is a big danger in schools today.'

---

Do not turn to the next page until you have attempted this exercise

---

## Exercise 32: Suggested Answers

There might be many ways of expressing a simplification of that passage. Here is one:

'The front left wheel of a motor car is excellent and essential to the functioning of a car. But by itself the front left wheel is not enough. In the same way, critical thinking is necessary for the functioning of society but it is not, by itself, enough. There is also a need for productive thinking.'

Or another:

'A car with brakes and a steering-wheel will not get very far if there is no engine, no fuel and no accelerator. By itself critical thinking has no energy for progress.'

Sometimes a simple choice of words can make a complex situation easier to understand. An analogy is sometimes a way of simplifying a relationship or a point that is being made.

# EXERCISE 33

How would you express in as simple a way as possible the arguments put forward in the following passage?

'Experiments have shown that when a person believes that he or she is deciding to do something the brain has already made that decision some time before. What does this say about free will? Free will is the basis of society. Religion and law are based on the exercise of free will. It is this exercise of free will which merits reward (in heaven) or punishment (in prison or in hell). Without the concept of free will society could not function.

'Quite apart from the experiments mentioned above, there is a feeling that upbringing, genes, hormones, chemicals in the brain, past experiences, role models, etc., all add up to pressures that force someone to act in a certain way. So how free are we really?'

---

Do not turn to the next page until you have attempted this exercise

---

## *Exercise 33: Suggested Answers*

There could be a lot of debate and discussion about how to summarize the passage. One possibility is as follows:

'In practical terms the illusion of free will is just as workable as the reality.'

# Lists

There are some people who introduce 'a', 'b' and 'c' into all their conversations. These might be factors, alternatives, choices, reasons, types, etc. This can be annoying because the listener feels an obligation to remember the listing. It can therefore be very irritating.

From time to time, however, there can be a clarifying value in offering a list as a list. If the items are simply run off in general conversational mode they may not get the attention they deserve. Items on a list are more clearly separated out and can therefore be seen to be more distinct. Each item can then become a point for discussion and examination. The distinctiveness of the different points would be lost in a general description.

A list is a powerful form of attention-directing both from the point of view of the person compiling the list and also from the point of view of the people to whom the list is presented. They may want to add to the list. They may want to claim that some points are not really separate but are aspects of the same thing.

So in spite of the sometimes irritating nature of 'listing' there can be a clarifying value.

# EXERCISE 34

From the following passage try to put together a 'list' of the possible explanations.

'Engineering should be the one profession that is open to creativity. You can test out ideas on a piece of paper, on a computer model or on a prototype. This immediate testing is not possible in most areas (medicine, law, economics, sociology, etc.). Yet in my experience engineers have the hardest time with creativity. Perhaps people go into engineering because they like everything to be definite and logical. Everything can be measured, worked out and predicted. Uncertainty is much reduced. There are laws and mathematics. In the advertising world success is at first subjective – you think it is a good idea. Then success is tested in the market. If the idea is not very successful then there is no huge disaster. Quite rightly engineers are trained to be competent. They must know how to do things the right way. If a box bridge collapses that is serious and dangerous. So competence is very important. It is the role of the educator to be sure that the students have this competence. The area of creativity is full of ambiguity, uncertainty, speculation and provocation. These are not the elements of engineering thinking. Yet when engineers see the logic of creativity (as essential behaviour in a self-organizing information system) they become very good at the creative game.'

---

Do not turn to the next page until you have attempted this exercise

---

## *Exercise 34: Suggested Answers*

It is possible that engineers are not creative for the following reasons:

1. The cost and consequences of failure in engineering are much higher than in 'creative' professions so there is an aversion to taking risks.

2. Engineering education is towards competence – towards doing things the way they should be done.

3. Those people who choose to go into engineering do so because they want certainty and logical progression from one point to the next.

4. The thinking idiom of engineering is very different from the thinking idiom of creativity.

5. No one has bothered to point out to engineers the 'logical' basis of creativity and how to play the creative game.

## Summaries

Summaries may be used at the end of a discussion or at any point along the discussion.

'Where are we at?'

'How far have we got?'

'What have we covered?'

'What are the main points again?'

From the point of view of 'interest' there is no need to be pedantic or heavy-handed about summaries. Nor is there any need for the summary to seek to be totally comprehensive. It is enough that the summary covers some of the main points and gives the general flavour of what has happened.

A summary may simply record different points of view.

'So we agree to disagree. This is your point of view . . . and this is my point of view . . . The difference arises from the different way in which we see people reacting to the suggestion.'

'It is clear that we have different values here. Your value is . . . and my value is . . . So we cannot agree.'

'Under these circumstances . . . what you see is correct. But under these other circumstances . . . what I say may be correct. It depends on the actual circumstances we find.'

# EXERCISE 35

Write a very short summary of Part 2 of this book. Then turn to the next page.

## Exercise 35

Part 2 of the book has been concerned with the basic thinking operations which we can use deliberately in order to generate and explore interest. These are mental activities which we can set out to do. They may be deliberate at first but may become habits eventually. They form part of the skill of 'interest'.

# PART 3

# THE DRIVERS OF INTEREST

### Feelings

Feelings provide the fuel for interest. There is a whole range of human feelings. They are there to be enjoyed. Interest seeks to draw in those feelings.

### Relevance

Relevance to yourself. Relevance to other people. Relevance to human nature and so on to individuals. Relevance is a key part of interest. Something becomes interesting as soon as it can be made relevant.

### Human Interest

There are a number of basic 'human-interest' drivers: sex, money, scandal, categories, etc. People are interested in people and people's behaviour.

### Emotions

These are the strong emotions. What is their place in 'interest'? Do they help with interest or do they interfere with interest? Emotions may be simple or mixed.

### Humenes

This is a new word to cover that aspect of interest that derives from physiological behaviour in the mind: humour, insight, surprise, etc. This is a powerful form of interest but need not involve either relevance or feelings.

## Fascination

A powerful form of interest. The interest that is aroused by wildlife television programmes. Something may be fascinating in itself. The importance of curiosity.

## Knowledge and Stories

The content part of interest. Information and experiences. First-hand or second-hand stories. The ingredients of interest as distinct from the operations.

# FEELINGS

Fishermen go out to catch fish. They are judged to be successful or otherwise according to the number of fish they catch.

Art, literature, drama, opera, soap operas and 'interest' are all attempts to catch 'feelings'.

I intend to separate out 'feelings' into three main groupings.

1. Feelings in general

2. Emotions

3. 'Humenes'.

You will not know what 'humenes' are and no dictionary will tell you. It is a word I invented because there is a huge need to invent such a word. It covers the variety of 'mechanical emotions' which arise from the way the mind works. There will be a specific section on it later.

## The Red Hat

In the Six Hats system of parallel thinking, the Red Hat allows a participant at the meeting to express his or her feelings as they exist. There is no need to explain, justify, qualify or apologize for the feelings. The Red Hat legitimizes feelings. They are a useful ingredient in a discussion.

Intuition and feelings can be based on experience in the field which gives rise to a gut feeling which might be difficult to itemize. Nevertheless, that feeling has validity and is a contribution.

This does not mean that intuition is always right. Intuition can be seriously wrong at times.

When they told Einstein about Heisenberg's proposed 'uncertainty principle', Einstein declared that his intuition insisted that the theory was wrong: 'God does not play dice.' It seems that Heisenberg was right and the great Einstein intuition was wrong.

Feeling is the fuel of interest. Without feeling there is boredom. Feeling is the key to interest.

How do we appreciate a good wine? We try to develop a palate for wine. We practise 'directing our attention' to different aspects of the taste. There is the bouquet. Then there are the different parts of the mouth and the tongue. We develop a vocabulary (fruity, fresh, flinty, etc.). Some of this is pretentiousness but some has a real value.

Which is the more important: wine tasting or our human feelings? Probably the feelings. But we make no effort to develop a palate (or palette) for human feelings. We are content to rely on crude passions and emotions: 'I like it' and 'I hate it.' We are misled into believing that unless feelings are strong enough to be passions or emotions then they have no value. This is nonsense. There are a lot of very valuable and far more subtle feelings. We need to notice them and to develop them.

It is this development of feeling that adds to interest. It is rather hard to see how someone who has no feelings could be interested in anything other than in directions for finding the lavatory.

Just as people learn to recognize and name a variety of flowers if they are keen gardeners, so we should be able to recognize and name and express a wide variety of feelings in order to be able to enjoy them. Leaving the feelings lurking unrecognized in the subconscious might be useful for the practice of psychoanalysis but not for anything else.

# EXERCISE 36

For each of the following items write down your feelings. Imagine you are wearing the Red Hat and are asked to express feelings on each of the items. Do not pause to consider what politically correct feelings you should have but put down the feelings as they exist. Go beyond simple 'like' or 'dislike' to discover and describe a richer variety of feelings.

1. Pupils at school to give a report on their teachers

2. A new tax on being overweight

3. Public-opinion polls

4. The monarchy

5. Unemployed people being required to do some work

6. A pension for poets

7. Marriage as a ten-year contract

8. Pre-nuptial agreements regarding property division on divorce

9. Single terms for politicians

10. On-the-spot fines collected and kept by policemen

11. A fine for littering the street

12. Legalizing soft drugs

13. Smoking ban in all public places

14. Promotion only by age, not by ability

15. Schools to teach constructive thinking as a basic subject

---

Do not turn to the next page until you have attempted this exercise

---

## *Exercise 36: Suggested Answers*

Obviously, feelings are very subjective. Below is an expression of some feelings about the issues.

1. Excellent idea, some danger of abuse.

2. Good intention, difficult to make fair or practical.

3. Very good. Too under-used in politics. Should have some political power.

4. Better than many other heads of state but could be improved.

5. Yes – if well organized.

6. Certainly.

7. Uncertain. Some merits. Practical difficulties with children. Probably happens that way anyway.

8. Not romantic but necessary.

9. Risk of losing the experienced ones. Perhaps a way could be devised of over-riding this with a very high vote.

10. Good idea provided no abuse.

11. About time.

12. A weak approach to the problem.

13. Only when the smoke affects others. Perhaps detectors to monitor the level of smoke.

14. Has a lot of merit provided there is a bypass for exceptional talent.

15. Astonishing that they are not already doing it routinely.

In the exercise responses, qualifiers and conditions have been inserted in some of the responses. This is acceptable for this exercise but not in a strict Red Hat use, which asks for a response to things as suggested.

## Examination of Feelings

Introspection means looking inward to examine feelings. It is not my intention to encourage 'navel gazing'. One of the ingredients of interest is, however, to be able to have feelings and to talk about them.

Feelings can be just as much a subject for discussion as the latest football scores or the latest gossip.

Most people, rightly, hate being asked what their feelings are on a specific subject. This is because they have not made those feelings visible to themselves – or they suspect those feelings are going to be used as a basis for manipulation (which is too often the case).

# EXERCISE 37

Examine and express your feelings on the following passage.

'The two most important philosophical statements of the twentieth century were made by Henry Ford and Groucho Marx.

'Henry Ford said of his Model-T that people could have any colour they wished – so long as it was black. (The reason was that black paint dried much more quickly than other colours.) This means that you will be perfectly happy and satisfied if what you want is exactly what is available to you.

'At the other extreme there was Groucho Marx who said, "I would never want to belong to any club which would consider having me as a member." This covers the yearning for something which is impossible to acquire.

'On the one hand there could be the contentment of a cow. On the other hand the perpetual striving of an artist towards an impossible perfection.

'Between the two extremes everyone should seek to place themselves somewhere along the spectrum. Where would you place yourself?'

---

Do not turn to the next page until you have attempted this exercise

---

## Exercise 37: Suggested Answers

The clarity of the two extremes creates an awkward tension. Both are seen to have value and both are seen to be limiting. The feeling is that one should have something of both positions. Perhaps there should be a solid base of contentment from which the striving takes place. There is also a feeling that perhaps we place too much emphasis on achievement and that contentment should not be despised.

## Views, Opinions and Feelings

Feelings may be expressed as such or they may be embedded in a view. Racist feelings are usually embedded in a view or opinion. The feeling that criminals are too cosseted is expressed in demands for tougher sentencing.

Prejudices against women in business are sometimes expressed through opinions on the need to look after a family, female physiology or the supposed use of female charm.

The proof that an opinion is merely a feeling in disguise is given by the generality of the opinion. If 'all' women are incompetent and 'all' the unemployed are scroungers, then it is clear that a feeling is at work.

While the having and expressing of feelings is an important part of interest, the simple parade of strong feeling is not particularly interesting except to show that such feelings exist. There is usually little room for exploration or discussion.

There is a simple test question that can be used:

'Are you content with that opinion?'

If the answer is 'yes' then there is little room for exploration.

# EXERCISE 38

Lay out the possible views of the following people on the following situation.

A company is reducing its full-time staff but is increasing its part-time staff. These are mainly women who find that the shorter hours fit in with their family demands. Part-time workers do not get the full benefits of full-time workers and have less job security. They are not represented by the same union as full-time staff.

Lay out the views of:

1. The management of the company

2. The union organizer

3. Part-time staff newly employed

4. A militant feminist

5. A laid-off full-time worker.

---

Do not turn to the next page until you have attempted this exercise

---

## *Exercise 38: Suggested Answers*

1. Part-time staff are cheaper. They are much more motivated. They can be increased or decreased to meet fluctuating demand. If the company is going to continue to exist it must be profitable and to do this it must cut its costs. A necessity.

2. This is the beginning of a dangerous trend. Full-time workers are being betrayed. The company has a responsibility to its workers, not just its shareholders. Part-time workers are being exploited since they are desperate for a job. The influence of the union will be reduced. Management needs to be shown that this sort of policy is not acceptable.

3. Grateful for a work opportunity that fits individual needs. A sense that possibly there is some exploitation. Sympathy for the full-time staff laid off. Some understanding of management thinking. Why shouldn't women with families be able to find suitable work?

4. The women are being exploited because of their need for work. Why should they not have full benefits and security? Is this a shift from male workers to female workers because these cost less? Having a family should not put women at a work disadvantage.

5. Very angry that management has no loyalty to existing staff. Resentment that 'cheaper' labour is taking the jobs. Women should not be prepared to work at lower pay and with fewer benefits. A gloomy outlook if others follow the same policy.

## **Other People's Shoes**

To give your own point of view is always of some interest. To be able to explore the point of view of others is of even more interest. This needs to be done honestly. You need to put yourself in the other person's shoes. If it is done badly it is worse than useless because it can give a false impression of the feelings of others.

A 'logic bubble' is that bubble of perceptions, values and feelings within which each person acts perfectly logically. The exercise is to try to see into that logic bubble.

The attempt is not to lay out what other people 'should' feel but what they might actually feel. Nor is it a matter of telling what you would feel in the other person's shoes. It is what the other person feels – with that person's intelligence, experience and background. When applied to other people the concept of 'ought' has no value.

Part of the exercise is to identify the different people in the situation who might have feelings on the matter.

## EXERCISE 39

Lay out the views and feelings of the different people involved in the following situation.

A young woman has taken on a new job which she finds very stressful. In particular she finds it difficult to deal with her immediate boss. The woman's boyfriend finds that she is depressed, irritable and difficult to be with. He suggests that she go to see his doctor. She goes to the doctor and asks to be put on Prozac, which she has read about. The doctor is not ready to do this but gives her a prescription for some pills.

She takes the pills and finds she is feeling much better. She can sleep at night and can deal with her boss. Her boyfriend is very pleased with the improvement.

One day she runs out of pills and finds that the doctor who prescribed the pills is away. In desperation she goes to another doctor. The other doctor tells her the pills were just vitamins. She is very upset.

Lay out the views and feelings of the people involved.

---

Do not turn to the next page until you have attempted this exercise

## *Exercise 39: Suggested Answers*

1. The first doctor is very upset because his placebo treatment was working well up to the point where the second doctor wrecked it.

2. The young woman is upset both at being deceived and also at having the deception lifted, because she can no longer believe in the pills. She is back to square one.

3. The boyfriend feels that he has been let down by the first doctor. He also resents the behaviour of the second doctor. He finds his girlfriend difficult to be with again.

4. The second doctor feels that he has stuck to his principles of not deceiving a patient. He cannot see why explaining that the pills were just vitamins did not convince the woman that she did not really need treatment.

5. The boss is puzzled as to why his assistant is back to her old difficult self. He wonders if it is anything he has done.

Some people feel that black and white photography was really more artistic than full-colour photographs. Everything had to be captured in tones of dark and brightness. It is the same with feelings. They add the depth, perspective and modelling to what we think and talk about. That is why an exploration of the nuances of feeling is such an important part of the interest process.

# RELEVANCE

Nothing is of interest unless it is relevant.

There is one big exception to this rule and that is the 'humenes' which I shall consider in a later section.

In general interesting things are relevant in some way to those who are interested.

Direct personal relevance is somewhat rare. Relevance usually comes through the 'human race' or through a 'special situation'.

Where something can be seen to be relevant to humanity in general then it becomes relevant to those humans discussing the matter. The transference from animals or insects to human behaviour is easily made even if scientifically very doubtful. Interest, unfortunately, is not only based on good science. Anything that happens with living creatures can be seen as a 'model' for human behaviour.

Personal situation relevance refers to situations like courting, marriage, aggression, group behaviour, etc. The transfer is from behaviour in those situations to the situation in which at least one of those discussing the matter happens to be.

# EXERCISE 40

What relevance to humanity might be claimed from the following examples?

'After mating the female house spider wraps its mate in a cocoon made from its web material and then proceeds to eat its mate at leisure.'

'While the male praying mantis is in the process of making love the female nonchalantly starts to eat him from the head down.'

Do not turn to the next page until you have attempted this exercise

## Exercise 40: Suggested Answers

1. The female of the species is much deadlier than the male.

2. The male is just a stud required for procreation services and is then entirely dispensable.

3. Passion has a curious way of showing itself.

4. Women get married and then proceed to 'consume' their husbands.

5. Maybe the female is so possessive she does not want the mate's genes to be spread elsewhere?

6. The male seems very docile in going to his fate. Maybe husbands are the same.

All these transferences are very far-fetched and have no biological basis whatsoever. But from the point of view of interest the extreme nature of the 'analogy' makes it more interesting. It would have been very weak and much less interesting to claim that 'women sometimes dominate their husbands'.

# EXERCISE 41

Note down the points of interest and relevance in the following example.

'When two prairie voles of opposite sex meet they make love for forty hours. Then they are chemically locked on to each other for ever in a sort of mutual obsession.'

---

Do not turn to the next page until you have attempted this exercise

---

## *Exercise 41: Suggested Answers*

1. Does the obsession arise from the lengthy lovemaking or the other way around? Is some bonding chemical released during human lovemaking?

2. Could we extract this 'bonding chemical' and give it to humans to make them bond for ever with computer-selected mates?

3. Is permanent mutual obsession better than the fickleness of traditional love?

4. What do different people feel about love compared to obsession?

5. One-sided obsession is not much fun, but what about mutual obsession?

In real life it is very interesting to note how sharply people divide between those who think that mutual obsession is the perfect answer to human romance and those who think it would be awful and restricting.

## **Remote Relevance**

In many instances the relevance is direct and the transfer to the human condition is obvious (even if unjustified). At other times the relevance is not immediately obvious and it is a duty of 'interest' to make the bridge and to show possible relevance. Poets do this all the time with their similes and metaphors. A skilled person can construct a relevance from almost any starting-point back to human nature.

This can be done through concept extraction, processes, similarity, opposites, etc.

'We can see a parallel here . . .'

'Contrast this with human behaviour . . .'

'There is an interesting concept here . . .'

The question to ask yourself is: 'How could this be a metaphor for human behaviour?'

In such exercises a good deal of latitude and poetic licence is allowed. Often it is the use of the item as much as its characteristics which permits the transfer of relevance.

# EXERCISE 42

The following five words were obtained randomly. For each word construct a relevance that makes some comment about human nature and human behaviour. The purpose of the exercise is not simply to make a link but to use the word as a metaphor.

For example if the word was 'bucket' the relevance might be as follows:
Those people who are continually taking things in and never reacting. One day they just spill over. They have had enough. We should not imagine that nothing is happening in the minds of the 'quiet ones'.

*The words:*

stink

factory

press

hammer

goat

---

Do not turn to the next page until you have attempted this exercise

---

## Exercise 42: Suggested Answers

### 'stink'

A stink is much more than a smell. A smell is there but a stink positively assaults you. At what point is the crossover? At what point does a smell become a stink? There are people who are nasty and unpleasant. Often we can live with them by ignoring them or overlooking their bad qualities. But there are other people who are in the 'stink' category. Their unpleasantness intrudes and cannot be ignored. What are the characteristics of such people? Why are they so unpleasant?

### 'factory'

Factories do the same thing over and over again. There is a productive routine. Maybe routines are productive. How much of life should be routine and how much should be novelty? Many people enjoy the comfort of the routine of everyday life because this allows them the joy of occasional deviations and adventures. Are routines necessarily boring? Any sport is a number of routines put together in novel ways.

### 'press'

This is taken to mean a trouser press, book press or duck press rather than the newspaper industry (that would also be valid). So pressure is applied in order to achieve the desired effect. When is pressure useful? Children are supposed to be brought up in total freedom instead of under the old-fashioned pressures. When is it necessary to exert pressure to make something happen? Do people really change their behaviour unless there is some pressure? Why do we always think of 'pressure' as a bad thing?

### 'hammer'

A hammer is a very powerful tool but it is totally useless without nails. The nail actually does the permanent work. The hammer simply puts the nail in the right position to do the work. So a hammer is a form of energy investment. Heavy investment over a short period gives a permanent effect. How willing are people to make investments that require a lot of effort in order to enjoy future benefits? Going to university or studying for exams might be examples. What other situations are there?

'goat'

The male goat is a very strongly masculine creature – much more masculine than a bull. It is not surprising that the Greeks made Pan a goat-like figure. What goes into this strong masculinity? It is not just threat of physical violence. There is a sort of dignity and disdain. The billy-goat is very clear about his position. Contrast this with the strutting of human machismo where there is a constant need to emphasize masculinity. The dignity of the goat is usually completely absent in human males.

## Show Relevance

The effort to show relevance is a key part of the interest process. Things which have no relevance simply flow by – unless they are humenes.

At any moment there needs to be an effort to link things back in. Why or how is this relevant? What can we learn from this? What does this tell us? This is not an educational effort because some of the transfers may be extreme. But connecting and linking things up is part of their interest, as discussed in a previous section.

# HUMAN INTEREST

People are interested in people. They are interested in how other people behave. They are interested in how they behave themselves. They are interested in general human behaviour. They are interested in the gossip about the mythical figures of celebrity.

Gossip is so strong, so reliable and so well-used a method of interest that I shall assume that it would be superfluous to write about it here. The gossip amongst a group of people all of whom know the subjects of the gossip is evidence of powerful interest at work. Often there is the element of a continuing drama with the pull of a television soap opera. What happens next? What did he do? What did she do? There is intrigue and curiosity. Gossip is a trading currency of human relations. You offer some gossip and expect to get some back. That gossip can be dangerous, damaging and unfair is all true, but then a kitchen knife can also be used for stabbing someone.

What I want to consider in this section are examples of those instances where the 'human interest' aspect is direct and does not have to be transferred. The relevance is obvious.

# EXERCISE 43

List and comment on the interest points in the following passage.

'It seems that mice can smell the "immune experience" of other mice. They choose to mate with mice whose immune experience is very different from their own. This is both a way of mating with mice who are not related and not part of the family, and also a way of ensuring that the offspring might get immunity from a much larger range of illnesses. There is some evidence to show that humans do exactly the same. They choose to mate with persons who have a completely different immune history (exposure to illness). It also seems that this choice mechanism is totally upset by the contraceptive pill. Under the influence of that pill women seem to choose persons with a more similar immune history.'

Do not turn to the next page until you have attempted this exercise

## Exercise 43: Suggested Answers

1. How we choose our mates is always of continuing interest.

2. Interesting to note that smell plays such an important part. Nor does it seem to be pheromones.

3. Should humans then be attracted to people from different areas and races where the immune history might be totally different?

4. If the pill messes up this selection system then a marriage formed while the bride was taking the pill might fall apart when she stopped taking it.

5. If two people were attracted to each other while the woman was not on the pill might they dislike each other when she was on the pill?

6. How do these chemical effects work in with the apparently psychological effects of 'liking'? Do the chemicals make the first decision and then psychology catches up with and rationalizes the decision?

This example is clearly of different interest to most people. Were their own marriages influenced in this way? What about the marriages which went wrong?

# EXERCISE 44

List and comment on the interest points in the following passage.

'A geneticist in Australia has claimed that "intelligence" is linked to the X chromosome. This means that intelligence in boys always comes from the mother. Girls get an X chromosome from both father and mother.'

Do not turn to the next page until you have attempted this exercise

## *Exercise 44: Suggested Answers*

1. Maybe this is why some cultures, such as the Jewish culture, place far more emphasis on the mother than on the father?

2. Does this mean that men should marry intelligent bluestockings rather than pretty air-heads?

3. Does this mean that girls have twice as much chance of being intelligent as do boys (X chromosome from either parent)?

4. Would girls be more intelligent than boys or would it even out because intelligent mothers would have intelligent sons?

5. If there are a lot of intelligent men around does it suggest that the intelligence of women has been underrated?

6. What do we mean by intelligence anyway?

7. Which X chromosome does the girl pass on to her son? The one inherited from her father or the one from her mother? Is it random? Should we look at the maternal grandfather?

8. This item is of interest because it combines the interest of both marriage and intelligence. There is also the element of 'practical action'. In addition it is possible to look around at others and oneself in order to seek to verify this claim.

An item of direct human interest engages people's thinking immediately. They see it affecting themselves and others around them.

People are interested in astrology because it gives them a framework to think and talk about themselves and also about their friends. Whether the predictions are true or not is less important. You can always select out those aspects which seem to make them true. A Taurus man can always be seen to be dependable and reliable.

There are always several levels of human interest:

1. Yourself

2. Those close to you

3. Others in the conversation

4. People known to those in the conversation

5. Celebrity samples of humanity

6. Humanity in general.

# EXERCISE 45

Pick out the human-interest points from the following passage.

'A friend of mine who keeps ducks tells me that there are apparently three distinct types of mating behaviour. One type of duck mates for life. If the mate dies the duck does not remarry. Another type of duck gets together with a mate for the season and the family of that season. Next season each chooses a different mate. A third type of duck goes in for one-night stands and casual mating.'

Why is this information (if it is indeed valid) interesting? What are the 'human-interest' points?

---

Do not turn to the next page until you have attempted this exercise

---

## *Exercise 45: Suggested Answers*

1. When we talk about some behaviour being natural and other behaviour being unnatural what do we mean? Maybe it is all natural if you choose your model.

2. Is this behaviour 'hard-wired' into the ducks? Is it built into their instincts and brains so that they have no choice? Is it possible that people are also programmed in different mating patterns? So that each person should follow their own pattern?

3. How did these different patterns evolve? Do they have special survival value?

4. From a species point of view is the casual mating best because the good genes get a better spread?

5. In the human race would men and women be equally happy with the different mating styles? Children need longer care than do ducks.

Categories and differences are always a strong source of interest. Into which box do I fit? Into which box does he fit? Whom am I similar to? Whom am I different from? Are we together in the same box? Who do we know who fits in that other box?

# EXERCISE 46

What are the human-interest points in the following piece?

'There is a part of Indonesia where women buy husbands. If you fancy a man you go along to the family and make an offer. If the offer is accepted you pay the money and have yourself a husband. In that region only women can own property.'

---

Do not turn to the next page until you have attempted this exercise

## *Exercise 46: Suggested Answers*

1. It would seem to be a feminist's paradise. How did it come about? How does it function, day to day?

2. What do the men think about it?

3. What happens thereafter in the family? Does the wife boss the husband around? Does the wife complain that she made a poor purchase?

4. What happens if two women want the same man? Is there an auction?

5. Does the man have any say in it at all?

6. Is the husband discarded if he proves useless? Can he be resold (at a bargain price)?

This example is so totally contrary to most cultures that it provides endless interest and speculation.

As usual it is the 'richness' around a subject that provides the interest. This richness can derive from a 'rich' starting-point or from the special elaboration efforts that are made around a poor starting-point. A rich starting-point full of human interest is ideal.

# EXERCISE 47

As before, read the following passage and pick out the 'interest' points.

'In India there is the custom that when a daughter gets married the family have to provide her with a dowry or promise money to the groom. If a family have many daughters they can be ruined. That may be why 90 per cent of illegal abortions are on girl babies. Yet in other cultures the groom has to pay the family of the bride in order to marry her. In South Africa the bride price is the *imbola*. One highly educated young woman had difficulty getting married because any prospective groom would have had to pay two hundred head of cattle. In the Middle East a good bride might cost $30,000. So it is usually cheaper to marry a Western woman who costs nothing (at first).'

Do not turn to the next page until you have attempted this exercise

## *Exercise 47: Suggested Answers*

1. What are the underlying reasons for this sharp division between cultures?

2. Does this difference lead to corresponding differences in the relationship between husband and wife?

3. What are the economic factors involved, both now and historically?

4. Very unfair on men or women who cannot afford to get married.

5. What are the equivalents, if any, in other cultures?

6. Which of the two systems is more appealing (or less unappealing) to women?

Many of the examples used here are to do with marriage and the relationship between the sexes. This is an obvious and much-used 'human interest' source. Cultural differences are not only interesting in themselves but provide a contrast so that we can look at our own customs in a different way. Instead of assuming that everyone does things in the same way we can see our own culture as only being one amongst many. So we may come to see some of our own practices as quaint and special instead of routine and sensible.

# EXERCISE 48

Pick out the human-interest points from the following passage.

'A clever person who commits a crime is somewhat less likely to be caught than a stupid person. Any person who commits a crime has to believe that he or she will not be caught. A clever person might have more fear of being caught than a stupid person so more stupid people commit crimes. A clever person can often find a way of earning a living honestly. A stupid person finds this difficult, especially with high inner-city unemployment. A stupid person is more likely to be led astray by his fellows and to join them in crime. So, for all these reasons, when we are punishing crime are we not really punishing stupidity? If so, is that fair, since this may be genetically determined?'

Do not turn to the next page until you have attempted this exercise

## Exercise 48: Suggested Answers

1. There is an element of truth in the argument and it does seem unfair.

2. Even if it is unfair there is not much that can be done about it in a practical sense.

3. Perhaps we could publicize widely the chances of getting caught in order to deter stupid people. In many types of crime the chances are probably so low that such publicity would actually encourage far more people to commit crimes.

4. The traditional difficulty of separating out the background reasons, factors, contributions, causes of criminal behaviour from the crime itself.

5. Is there any evidence that people who commit crime are of a lower intelligence? (At least the ones who are caught?)

6. Life is unfair to people of lesser intelligence and this is just one more example.

You only have to look at any tabloid newspaper to find out the main drivers of human interest: money, sex, crime, scandal, disaster, royalty and lost dogs.

# EMOTIONS

Rather surprisingly, emotions do not play a strong part in 'interest'. Feelings are more important. The reason is that emotions are so strong that they dominate the situation and kill the interplay, exploration and elaboration that is so essential to interest. A person in the grip of a strong emotion may be interesting in himself or herself but does not contribute to an interesting discussion.

There is one aspect of emotion which does contribute to interest. It is to do with shock, horror, disgust, voyeurism and prurience. People do seem interested in the details of disasters, serial killings, torture, strange sex practices, etc.

Some of this interest may be curiosity. In the case of plane crashes or terrorism there may be the sense of 'it could have happened to me'.

The attraction of horror and unpleasantness is not easily explained but is easily exploited. It may be that people see themselves as leading such humdrum lives that anything exotic suggests that there is 'out there' another type of life. Just as you might be interested in the tales told by someone who has just returned from an exotic country, so you might be interested in other 'exotic' behaviour. The abnormality is the basis of the interest. A murderer who kept parts of his victims in the freezer and ate bits from time to time seems more interesting than a drunk driver who kills a pedestrian.

As with gossip this source of interest is traditional and does not need much elaboration here. Whether one approves of it or not is unlikely to make any difference to its continuing as a powerful source of interest. Perhaps our interest in abnormality is really an affirmation of our appreciation that most of humanity is pretty normal.

# EXERCISE 49

What do you think the different emotional reactions might be to the suggestion made below?

'In the USA about 50,000 people a year are killed in road accidents. Sometimes there is a person at fault through drunk or careless driving. Sometimes a combination of circumstances or mechanical failure causes the accident. In all cases a "more or less" innocent person is killed. This is the price we pay for continuing to use cars and roads as a fundamental necessity in society. If everyone were to drive at five miles an hour there would be rather fewer accidents but life would be very difficult indeed.

'Suppose we consider crime as a "social accident". A number of circumstances have come together. Genes, upbringing, environment, peer pressure, lack of work, opportunity, etc., are all ingredients that have come together to cause this "social accident". As a result of this accident the criminal dies through capital punishment. It is not a matter of revenge or blame but the removal from society of someone who threatens society. Such an argument would lead to the extension of the death penalty – which would be carried out in the most humane manner.'

---

Do not turn to the next page until you have attempted this exercise

## *Exercise 49: Suggested Answers*

1. Horror and outrage. A motor accident is totally different since there is no intention to kill another human being.

2. In the suggestion someone is being killed because a combination of circumstances has put that person in a weak position.

3. Perplexity with the problem of those people who – even through no fault of their own – seem unable to live in society.

4. Favour the idea because too much sympathy is given to the criminal and not enough to the victims. It is too often seen that the victims are victims of 'accidents'.

5. Fear that this sort of thinking could lead to all sorts of barbarities carried out in the name of logic.

In this example strong emotions might be felt but would not be expressed as emotion but more as feelings and convictions.

There is a whole range of emotions which overlap with feelings. It is impossible to draw a category distinction between feelings and emotions as there is so much overlap. The simple distinction that emotions control our behaviour whereas feelings are only an ingredient in our behaviour does not always hold.

# EXERCISE 50

What sorts of emotion could be triggered by the following true story?

'In Italy a man who had reached his hundredth birthday was being given a party by his family and the villagers. His hat blew off in the wind. He chased after his hat and died of a heart attack.'

---

Do not turn to the next page until you have attempted this exercise

---

## *Exercise 50: Suggested Answers*

1. Sadness that such a joyous occasion should have been terminated in such a sad way.

2. Sadness that the triviality of chasing his hat should have brought to an end a magnificent life.

3. Sadness that no one had offered to run after his hat for him.

4. Perhaps that was the best way to die. Quickly and in the middle of a celebration. Much better than lingering for weeks with a fatal illness.

5. Sympathy for all those at the celebration party who must have been very upset.

Emotions can be gentle and yet strong at the same time.

# EXERCISE 51

Below is a list of five randomly obtained words. Try to see how and in what circumstances each of the 'words' could trigger an emotion. What would that emotion be?

letter

ladder

necktie

applause

poster

---

Do not turn to the next page until you have attempted this exercise

## Exercise 51: Suggested Answers

'letter'

A letter could be full of sad news. A son killed in a car accident. The death of a beloved grandmother. A letter could bring happiness. Acceptance of a marriage proposal. News of excellent examination results. A letter could bring news of an award, for example a knighthood. A letter may be one in an ongoing quarrel with another party. So the letter might excite anger and fury. A letter could arouse almost any emotion depending on the contents and circumstances.

'ladder'

The extension ladder of a fire truck to rescue people trapped by fire. Fear of the fire. Fear of climbing, or being carried, down the ladder. Fear of heights anyway in going up or down a ladder. Joy at a ladder used to rescue someone who had fallen into a pit and could not get out of it. Joy of a ladder as used in the traditional method of elopement.

'necktie'

Pride as someone admires your necktie. Anger as a wife dislikes the husband's choice of tie and tells him he has no taste. Fear as a tie is caught up in some revolving machinery and threatens a serious accident. Worry as a tie is used as a tourniquet to stop the bleeding from an injured arm. Pride as a growing lad puts on a tie for the first time.

'applause'

Pride, joy and satisfaction as applause greets the announcement that a political candidate has won an election. Applause at a theatre, concert, speech or athletic event. Disgust at the artificial applause in a television studio during an audience show. Horror at the applause when a French aristocrat had his head cut off by the guillotine. Disgust at applause in a theatre for a racist comment.

'poster'

Disgust at an obscene poster. Fear at the poster of a political rally supporting fascism or Marxism. Dismay at a poster encouraging young people to smoke. Sadness at a poster appealing for money to save starving children. Delight at a poster showing a beautiful man or woman. Delight at an old poster as a work of art.

## Mixed Emotions

There is a classic story about 'mixed emotions': seeing your mother-in-law drive over the cliff in your brand-new Mercedes.

Mixed emotions are far more interesting than unmixed emotions – because there is so much more going on in the mind. At one moment one emotion is dominant and then this gives way to another; then back to the first and so on. That is more interesting than the rigidity of single emotions.

# EXERCISE 52

Examine the different emotions involved in the following situation.

'The National Lottery in the UK has been very successful. People spend a lot of money on the lottery. Instead of just buying a ticket, the player chooses a set of numbers from 1 to 49. To some extent the success of the lottery depends on people's ignorance of mathematics. If a player gets two numbers right then he or she feels that much has been achieved. If three numbers are right then that player is halfway there and a little more effort might win the prize. This sense of achievement is based on a lack of understanding of the true mathematical probabilities.

'As the result of this lack of understanding the lottery authority makes a lot of money. Is this not trading on people's ignorance? Should that be allowed?

'At the same time this same ignorance gives players a much greater sense of fun, joy and achievement in doing the lottery. Even if falsely based, there is this sense of achievement. Perhaps that is what the purpose of a lottery is: to pay for an enjoyment of anticipation and achievement.

'So the key question is: should it be permissible to fool people for their own good? At the same time you are benefiting greatly from the fooling.'

---

Do not turn to the next page until you have attempted this exercise

---

## *Exercise 52: Suggested Answers*

1. The basic moral principle is 'the end does not justify the means'. So no matter how beneficial the end is to all parties this does not justify deception.

2. If people are getting more value for their money then how can this be bad?

3. The lottery organizers are interested in making more money through relying on 'ignorance'. This is a sort of deceit for their own gain.

4. There are no victims. Everyone is happy. So what is the problem?

5. Why would anyone be better off if players simply bought a ticket with an assigned number? There would not be the fun of choice and the fun of 'achievement'.

6. Once it is permitted to fool people even 'for their own good', then this opens the door to propaganda and all sorts of skilled deceits.

7. Governments fool people all the time. So what is different?

In this example the interplay of different emotions and different principles makes it interesting. There is also no easy answer.

# HUMENES

A friend of mine, Professor Ungku Aziz, found that the Bahasa language used in Malaysia did not have a word for 'mind'. So he invented the word *minda*, which is now in such general use that it even appears on advertising posters.

Although language seems so rich it is in fact very deficient in words to describe processes. That is why I had to invent the term 'lateral thinking' to describe the thinking involved in changing perceptions and concepts instead of just working with them. For the same reason I had to invent the word 'po' to signal a provocation. Without such a signal we would never know when a deliberate provocation was being offered.

We need new words to describe the following more succinctly:
'the way we look at things'
'running something forward in the mind'
'interest points'
'direct your attention'.

I invented the term 'logic bubble' to describe that total bubble of perceptions, emotions and values within which every person acts perfectly logically.

The word 'humene' is a new word that is also badly needed. In discussing interest, I have looked at interest arising from feelings, emotions, basic human interest and relevance. But there is a whole other class of interest which need not be connected at all to human interest.

The interest of humour arises directly from the physiological mechanisms in the brain. The humour may be totally remote and say nothing about the human condition, but it remains interesting.

The brain has a powerful mechanism for disliking what is different from what is expected. When Professor Bruner at Harvard made up a pack of playing-cards in which every card was normal with the exception of the three of hearts, he got some interesting results. His three of hearts was black instead of red. When students were asked to look through the pack, they would often feel nauseous or even be sick when they came to the black three of hearts. This mismatch mechanism can be very strong.

So quite apart from the usual emotions and feelings listed by psychologists there is a whole range of feelings that arise from the neuronal function in the brain.

At a tennis tournament there are 131 entrants for the singles event. How many matches would there need to be? It is not too difficult to work backwards from the end result: one match at the end, two in the semi-finals, four in the quarter-finals – and so on. There will also be some byes in the first round. But it is far simpler to see how many matches there would need to be to produce 130 losers (one winner). The simple answer is 130 matches since each match produces one loser.

Simple answers to apparently complex problems often produce laughter and a sense of pleasure. This is closely related to the laughter and pleasure of humour. The same mechanism applies to insight and 'eureka' moments (sudden flashes of insight).

By and large psychologists have neglected this important area of feeling and emotion because it does not seem to have the survival value of sex, hunger, thirst, aggression, etc. Yet in everyday life it is an even more important part of life than the 'heavy' emotions.

In the area of interest these 'mechanical' sources of interest are very central. Yet we do not seem to have a word to describe this whole class of feelings.

That is why it was necessary to invent the word 'humene'. It is obviously derived from 'humour'. It is intended to cover all those brain mechanisms which give a positive sense of pleasure or interest, just as humour does. 'Humene' was chosen in preference to 'humoid' for obvious reasons.

## Surprise

If something is different from our expectations we get a surprise. An infant will gurgle with delight at a surprise but react with horror to a fright. A surprise is something that at first is puzzling but then it suddenly makes sense – in exactly the same way as does humour. In humour there is a preposterous situation which is suddenly seen to be 'logical' in some way.

The angry passenger stormed into the stationmaster's office to complain that the two clocks on the platform showed differing times. Was that not incompetence?

'Not at all,' replied the stationmaster, 'what would be the use of having two clocks if they showed exactly the same time?'

There is a strange logic which we accept for the sake of humour.

A caricature has the same value. We are at first surprised by it but then relate it back, logically, to the person involved.

# EXERCISE 53

Give answers to the following questions.

1. Which country has the second-highest population in South America?

2. Which country has the highest rate of suicides under the age of twenty-four?

3. Where was the biggest shark caught?

4. Which two countries in Europe have the lowest birth rates?

5. If a child in a car is holding a helium-filled balloon on a string and the car goes round a sharp corner, which way does the balloon move relative to the car?

6. If you drop two equal-sized balls, one made of solid steel and the other made of solid wood, which one would hit the ground first?

---

Do not turn to the next page until you have attempted this exercise

## *Exercise 53: Suggested Answers*

1. The answer is Colombia. This surprises some people because Argentina is such a large country that it is supposed that it also has the second highest population after Brazil.

2. The answer is Australia. This is a huge surprise. Most people think of Japan or Sweden. Australia is such a big surprise because the quality of life in Australia is about the highest in the world. (It has to be said that many countries do not keep accurate statistics on suicides.)

3. The answer is ten miles north of Malta in the Mediterranean. This is a big surprise because most people would think of Australia or the Caribbean and would not think of the Mediterranean.

4. The answer is Spain and Italy. This again is a big surprise because both are Catholic countries and artificial methods of birth control are not supposed to be used.

5. The answer is that the balloon moves in towards the corner and not outwards. Ordinary centrifugal force might suggest it should move outwards. But the air in the car is heavier than the helium in the balloon so the air moves outwards forcing the balloon inwards.

6. The answer, of course, is that they both reach the ground at the same time. For 1500 years people believed that the heavier object would hit the ground first because the great Aristotle had said so. Then Galileo showed otherwise from the top of the Leaning Tower of Pisa. Actually, a fifteen-second thought experiment would give the same result.

(It has to be said that these answers are correct only at the time of writing this book and will not be correct for ever.)

A recent study on the nature of beauty showed a rather surprising finding. A series of beautiful faces were shown to students who were asked to rate them for beauty. The results suggested that regular features were necessary for beauty but that this was not enough. Apparently one feature had to be slightly exaggerated. A mouth that was bigger than normal. Eyes that were bigger than normal. A nose that was exaggerated. A higher forehead. A small chin. Just one feature needed to be exaggerated a little bit. This fits in the concept of 'surprise'. Something that is 'different' but also 'the same'.

Things that are 'bizarre' may become interesting for the same reason. It may also be that bizarre things simply catch attention.

## Expectation

Snooker apparently makes good television. There are the coloured balls and the green surface and seriousness of the participants and all that, but the main source of interest is 'expectation'. The viewer clearly sees what the player is trying to do. Then within a few seconds the player has or has not done it. This is the same sort of interest that is aroused by quiz shows. There is a set-up with a clear expectation. Then, within a few seconds, we see the result. Obviously, there do need to be a lot of successes in order to sustain the interest.

Interest can be engineered by 'setting things up'. This can be done by means of a question or by means of an offered choice.

'Which is more important to you: excitement or peace?'

'Which is the more useful: beauty or personality?'

'What would you have done at this point . . . ?'

A question is always a 'set-up'. Simple things put as questions can become more interesting.

# EXERCISE 54

Below are given five randomly obtained words. Around each word frame either a direct question or a choice question.

prize

park

traffic-lights

sandwich

stew

---

Do not turn to the next page until you have attempted this exercise

---

## Exercise 54: Suggested Answers

'prize'

Which of the following would you prefer as a prize:
1. A round-the-world cruise costing £10,000 (not saleable)
2. £5,000 in cash immediately
3. £600 a year for life (but taxable as income)?

Different answers and explanations would develop the interest factor.

'park'

Which is preferable: one very big park in a city or lots of smaller parks?

Reasons for the answer and the thinking behind it would open up interesting avenues.

'traffic-lights'

Could traffic-lights be abolished if there was some way of motorists organizing themselves at junctions?

Methods of doing this and the likelihood of motorists obeying the rules of the system are open to discussion.

'sandwich'

Which is the most important part of a sandwich? Is it the bread with added flavour? Or is it the filling supported by the bread? Is the bread really a sort of convenient container? Much would depend on the quality of the bread.

'stew'

Which taste do you prefer: the pure taste of good ingredients or blended tastes as in a stew or sauce?

The discussion opens up to consider tastes which should be pure and others which are better blended. How did different cuisines emerge? Were sauces invented to cover bland and decaying food?

# FASCINATION

Fascination is a very powerful source of interest. It is part of the 'humene' group. Something may be fascinating in itself even if it has no relevance to human behaviour. The interest is even stronger if the item is both fascinating and also has a relevance to human behaviour.

To be fascinating something must be unusual; logically coherent; and open up lots of questions. Fascinating means that moment-to-moment you want to see what happens next.

Wildlife programmes on television are interesting because they are fascinating. The bombardier beetle squirts very hot liquid at its enemies. How does it heat up the liquid? Why is it not damaged by its own heated liquid? How did it learn to do this? How effective is this weapon? It is fascinating because of the 'heat' element. Other creatures might squirt liquid, dye, acid or poison, but heat is unusual.

There is a frog in Queensland which swallows its own fertilized eggs. The eggs develop in the frog's stomach. When the little frogs are ready, the mother opens its mouth and the baby frogs jump out. This is fascinating because it is so bizarre and yet so logical.

How does the frog know to turn off the acid in its stomach so that the eggs are not simply digested? Researchers are indeed trying to isolate this factor to turn off human acid when people have ulcers in the stomach. How do the young frogs get their oxygen in the stomach?

What does the mother live on when she cannot do any eating? How long does the process take?

Finally, how did it all come about? It is difficult to see how traditional evolution would have brought about the conjunction of so many factors at once.

In Japan the word for 'thank you' is *arrigato*. This seems to have come from the Portuguese word *obregado*. Yet the Portuguese 'black ships' only arrived in Japan relatively recently. Did the Japanese have no word for 'thank you' before the Portuguese arrived? Why was this word taken up so readily? Were the Japanese just trying to be polite to the Portuguese visitors and then got stuck with the word?

The Italian *Panettone*, which is much eaten around Christmas, is made 'upside down'. It is a very light bread. When it cools after being baked the bread would naturally sink down so that it was less airy. But if the bread is put upside down then it actually sinks 'upwards' and retains its airiness.

How did birds ever develop wings to fly? A giraffe with a slightly longer neck would be able to get more food than other giraffes, so the long-necked giraffes would prosper because there was an immediate advantage as the neck grew longer and longer over time. This is easy to understand. But a bird's wings would be useless and would offer no advantage at all until they were big enough to support flight. So why should the wings have got bigger and bigger if there was no advantage? Put this way the simple fact that birds have wings becomes fascinating. What could have happened? Possibility and speculation open up the matter.

It is possible that wings started with sea birds. Birds like penguins and puffins use their wings to swim under water. The bigger the wing the better the swimming. So big-wing birds caught more fish. This gives the immediate advantage. Then one day a sea bird tumbled off a rock and learned to fly?

Or perhaps the evolution route came via flying reptiles.

# EXERCISE 55

What is interesting in the following passage? Try to identify the points of 'fascination'.

'In certain aboriginal languages in Australia there is a special separate language for a man to talk to his mother-in-law. It seems that in the past men were betrothed to girls who were very young. The man usually preferred the mother to the intended bride. To guard against this tendency the mother-in-law (to be) was made "taboo". This meant that ordinary language could not be used between them because this would have been contaminated by the taboo. So a special language had to be created.'

---

Do not turn to the next page until you have attempted this exercise

---

## Exercise 55: Suggested Answers

1. A fascinating example of the consequences of limited categories. If the mother was made 'taboo' then all else followed. If there had been some way of putting her 'out of bounds' without going so far as making her taboo, then there would have been no need for a separate language.

2. Does everyone use the special language to the mother? This would seem very unfair. Is it only the groom-to-be that must use that language with his mother-in-law-to-be? If there is a group it must be very awkward to have to keep switching languages depending on who is being addressed.

3. What other examples are there of different languages within the same culture? In Japan a woman's Japanese is very different from a man's Japanese. In other cultures the language with which you address a superior person is very different from the language you address to your equals.

4. Who teaches the young man and the mother this special language? Obviously, they could not just 'pick it up'. Whose business is it to know this language and to teach it?

5. Fascinating that for totally different reasons the mother-in-law in aboriginal culture and many other cultures is not part of the family group but is regarded as an outsider.

## Curiosity

Curiosity is a great driver of interest. No one seems quite sure how to classify curiosity. Is it a sort of emotion? The drive to find out and to explore? It probably fits under humenes.

You notice some flowerpots on a stone shelf above a door. What do they mean? You are curious. You find out that each flowerpot indicates an unmarried daughter. So traditionally a family signalled to the world outside that marriageable daughters were available.

Perhaps the young men then called or hung around hoping to meet the young ladies. Perhaps that is where the expression 'left on the shelf' originated?

There is a biological urge to explore unknown things to find out whether they are dangerous, neutral or good to eat. An infant is forever doing this with his or her mouth. There is a need to explore territory to discover good things and to become aware of dangers. In a more general sense this curiosity-driven exploration is a key ingredient in interest.

Some people's curiosity is immediately aroused. Such people can frame their own questions, which then open up interest. This can become a useful habit. Other people just seem to accept things as they are without any need to wonder or to ask questions. Such people need to have the questions framed for them and put before them. Then their interest is aroused and they also become eager to go further and to find answers to the questions.

## EXERCISE 56

Put together eight questions which might stimulate interest in the following phenomenon.

'In the bird world mating is usually on the basis of vanity. The female birds select the male bird with the longest tail feather or the brightest breast. These selected males get all the mating action. Perhaps that is why parrots live so long. A male parrot with the right feature would go on mating into old age. So a long-lived parrot would put more "long-life" genes into the population. Contrast this with animals who have to fight to get the females (stags, walruses, etc.). To fight you have to be young and fit. So fighting genes may get into the population but not long-life genes.'

---

Do not turn to the next page until you have attempted this exercise

---

## *Exercise 56: Suggested Answers*

The eight curiosity-stimulating questions might be:

1. Do the good looks of the male bird have any survival advantage?

2. What is the benefit of having one set of genes distributed more widely in the population rather than all the genes being distributed?

3. If the best females select the best-looking male does this mean that those 'best female' genes get continued on in the population?

4. Does it mean that in time all the male birds will be equally good-looking? How then would selection be made?

5. Species of birds with casual mating habits should live longer than faithful birds because the long-life genes would be more widely spread in the population. Would this happen?

6. What is the equivalent in the human population of vanity mating?

7. What is the difference if vanity mating is directed towards good-looking females rather than males? Males can have many more offspring than females.

8. Would any basis for 'focused mating' have the same effect?

Skill and imagination in framing questions provide the basis for interest. As a stimulating question is answered the subject has to be explored more fully with possibilities, speculation and evaluation. It is this exploration that creates fascination.

# KNOWLEDGE AND STORIES

At the beginning of this book I made it clear that special experiences, special interests and special jobs were all powerful sources of interest – but not the subject of this book. At the same time some knowledge, some information and some 'content' are necessary. It is true that you can simply respond with interest and speculation to information put out by others but from time to time you need to be the source of that information.

It is perfectly possible to have an interesting and intelligent conversation about books, plays, concerts and television programmes, with people who have had the same experience. This is one type of the 'special' experiences which I excluded at the beginning.

With regard to 'general information' it is possible to pick up a huge amount of information from ordinary newspapers and magazines. It is not so much the major stories that matter. It is the small, tucked-away paragraphs that are usually the most interesting. They may cover research findings (people who drink tea have less chance of getting a stroke), events or anecdotes. These little nuggets of information can be taken and put into your hoard.

It is important to 'read between the lines'. I have often found myself talking to someone who has read exactly the same article that I have read and I appeared to be telling that person new things. If you read carefully between the lines you can extract far more.

Why did this happen?

Why did this not happen?

Who would really have been affected?

What other background factors were there?

These are the general-interest questions which allow a reader to get far more from what is read. Interest is not only based on what you do with what you know, but also on how you get to know things. The questioning of interest is part of the reading process.

Why do some people remember things they have read and others do not? It is the difference between putting an ingredient on the shelf in the kitchen and actually cooking with the ingredient. If you note the 'interest' when you come across something, if you ask certain questions and if you make connections, then your 'use' of that information puts the information actively into your mind instead of just plonking it there passively.

After a while you can develop a habit of being 'sensitive' to interest. Just as a wine buff can detect a fine wine so an interest buff can detect the 'interest quality' of any item that has been read. You store the item under 'miscellaneous interest'. The more you then use the item the easier it gets to use it.

# EXERCISE 57

In the following list of twenty randomly obtained items are there any three about which you know something interesting?

| | |
|---|---|
| surf | milk |
| rhinoceros | hairdresser |
| debt | carpenter |
| shout | kangaroo |
| lie | chewing-gum |
| | |
| hard hat | laundry |
| scales | star |
| lock | snow |
| exam | bottle top |
| parachute | aqualung |

Put down the information you know on any three items.

---

Do not turn to the next page until you have attempted this exercise

## *Exercise 57: Suggested Answers*

Knowledge about any three of the items will vary from person to person. Here are some examples.

### rhinoceros

The rhinoceros horn is not really a horn at all but matted hair. Powdered rhinoceros horn is much prized by the Chinese as an aphrodisiac merely because it stands upright. The horn is also prized as a handle for ceremonial daggers. Rhinoceros are therefore killed just for their horns. Removing the horns in advance also removes the reason for killing the rhinoceros.

### lie

Surprisingly there is very little agreement amongst moral philosophers about lies. Is it permitted to tell a lie to save someone's life? Is it permitted to tell a lie in order to do good – as with a doctor prescribing a placebo? Some moralists have said that all lies under all circumstances are not permitted. Others have defined when it is permissible to tell a lie. There is a huge amount of debate on the subject.

### kangaroo

A kangaroo is 30 per cent more efficient than a horse. When a horse raises its body the horse gets none of that energy back. When a kangaroo hops some of the energy is stored in the 'springs'. Kangaroos could only develop the very strong muscles needed for hopping because they have very small pelvic outlets. The kangaroo baby is a very tiny 'Joey' which crawls up into the pouch, attaches itself to a nipple and goes on growing.

### chewing-gum

The Singapore government banned chewing-gum because youngsters were putting chewing-gum on the edge of the subway train doors, so preventing the doors closing and the train starting. It is also possible that the government wanted to show that if it could be bothered with chewing-gum it did not have any major problems.

snow

It is said that the Inuit have twenty words for different types of snow. If snow is a major part of your environment then you learn to distinguish different types even as a gardener distinguishes types of weed.

You can do this exercise yourself at any time. The words must, however, be truly random otherwise there is no point to the exercise.

Once your mind is full of items of information then some of these pieces can start to connect up, so generating 'necklaces' of interesting information.

# EXERCISE 58

What could the following item of information connect with?

'Crocodiles have the ability to change the sex of the crocodiles within the unhatched eggs. The eggs are laid on the river bank and covered with mud. If the mother chooses to sprinkle the mud with water the temperature of the eggs is lowered and the sex of the crocodile inside is changed.'

---

Do not turn to the next page until you have attempted this exercise

## *Exercise 58: Suggested Answers*

1. The effect of temperature on the sex of reptile eggs is sometimes suggested as a reason for the extinction of the dinosaurs, which were so very successful – lasting 65 million years. The suggestion is that a meteorite impact on the earth threw up clouds of dust which obscured the sun and led to cooler temperatures. The result was that the majority of dinosaur eggs were of the same sex and so the species died out.

2. The effect of temperature on reproduction may also be seen in humans. If men wear briefs that are very tight then the temperature in the testicles is too high and they become temporarily infertile.

3. As with the fish that change sex to keep a sex balance in the population, there must be some way of telling which sex is needed. What could that be?

Information does not always need to be first hand. Someone tells a good story. You make a note of that story and can then use it yourself later.

It is said that on leaving a party Oscar Wilde remarked to a friend that someone had made a very witty remark and that he, Oscar, wished he had said it himself.

His friend replied, 'You will, Oscar, you will.'

If you can acknowledge the source of the story so much the better but this can become complex.

The well-known urban myths are stories that circulate and circulate but have no basis in fact. They fit in with the Italian phrase *ben trovato* (good enough to be true). If you doubt the veracity of a story it is better not to pass it on.

The more implications which an item of information seems to

have the more interesting it can be. You will need to note these implications when reading the item in the first place and also when speaking about the item. All this is part of the 'richness' and 'elaboration' aspect of interest.

If we were to look at interest as a 'smell' then there are items which have a strong odour and items which have no odour. Those with a strong odour you can detect from a distance. The odour is what reaches out from the item itself. The odour represents the widening circle of interest that spreads around an interesting item.

# EXERCISE 59

In what way is the following item of interest? What are the implications?

'Epilepsy is uncontrolled brain activity which can lead to fits. The "limbic" part of the brain is said to control mood, anger, aggression, etc. Research has suggested that there is such a thing as "limbic epilepsy". This means that uncontrolled activity in this area can lead to sudden acts of extreme violence. The attacker suddenly "wakes up" and finds that he or she has committed some horrible act.'

Do not turn to the next page until you have attempted this exercise

## Exercise 59: Suggested Answers

The implications are huge for the whole area of crime and justice. If this finding is indeed correct then it would not be just to punish someone for a type of epilepsy over which he or she had no control. It might be difficult to prove this. The excuse could become used in all sorts of crimes of violence. How could it be medically detected?

If there is no simple cure then what should be done with such people? It may be no fault or choice of their own, but they are not 'fit' to live in ordinary society because of the danger to others. Yet if such attacks occurred only once or twice in a lifetime should such people be locked away for ever because of the risk of an attack?

The whole basis of crime, justice, society is challenged by this possibility.

# Stories

I am not referring here to major stories or personal-experience stories. As noted before, such stories can be a great source of interest but they are not available to those who have not had the experience.

At this point 'stories' refers to anecdotes, short stories and funny stories.

There are two key considerations:

1. They must be short

2. They must make a point.

There are indeed some natural storytellers who can sustain with interest a long-drawn-out story. Congratulations to them, because such stories can be very interesting. That skill, however, is not available to everyone and a long story without that skill is very boring.

The point of a story is that it should make a point. A story is not just permission to use up speaking time. A story is not just permission to impose your voice on the ears of others.

A story is a sort of extended metaphor or analogy. It tells something about human nature; about a particular person; about a particular culture; about a particular habit; or about a particular event. Accents, characterization and word pictures add tremendously to the value of the story but the mechanics of the story should be good.

# EXERCISE 60

Does the following story work? What are the key features? What is the point that is being made?

'At the end of a long morning of oral examinations, the professor says to the last student, "I can ask you all the usual questions or just one very difficult question. Just one question. Which do you choose?"

"The one difficult question."

The professor thinks for a while and then says, "Here is the question and it is very difficult. Which is the single most important thing in the whole of Western civilizaton?"

Without any hesitation at all the student replies:

"Chewing-gum."

"Why do you say chewing-gum?" asks the professor.

"You promised just one question," replies the student.

---

Do not turn to the next page until you have attempted this exercise

---

## *Exercise 60: Suggested Answers*

The story works best for those who know the academic world. The tyranny and pomposity of some professors get their come-uppance in the story. The student outsmarts the professor in a neat and logical way.

The neatness of the story is important and gives the story its bite.

The general point to be made is that if you are quick-witted, creative and smart you may be able to think yourself out of a difficult situation.

The story line is strong and uncomplicated and does not depend on special accents or effects. Anyone could tell the story.

So there are two main points:

1. The value of creative thinking

2. Authority is 'defeated'.

For their full effect stories rely on surprise, exaggeration, insight and humour. A good story makes full use both of the humenes and also of other feelings. For example the story would be even stronger if the professor's voice was imitated as being haughty and imperious. The turnaround would then be even more effective.

# EXERCISE 61

This is a very difficult exercise and you can skip it if you wish.

Below are five randomly obtained words. Choose any three of them to construct a story.

sheep

bell

prison

snake

laundry.

---

Do not turn to the next page until you have attempted this exercise

---

## *Exercise 61: Suggested Answers*

The laundry business was not going very well so the owner decided to start up an animal-washing service. Any sort of animal could be washed, from sheep to snakes. You could bring the animal to the laundry or the service would come to you. It was so successful that eventually the original laundry was closed down. One day someone decided to challenge the promise to wash even snakes and turned up with a snake. The laundry owner pulled the snake backwards into a long plastic tube and then proceeded to pull it out, tail first, inch by inch and to wash it. The challenge had been met.

# PART 4

# INTERACTION

## Discussion

Discussion and conversation. Interacting with other people. The use of the basic 'interest operations' to increase the interest of a discussion.

## Agreement

The value and use of agreement. Ways of agreeing. Developing and building on ideas. Full agreement and partial agreement.

## Disagreement

The dangers of negativity. The ego-driven sources of disagreement. The fundamental flaw in Western thinking. The benefits of parallel thinking. The Six Hats framework for discussion. Designing a way forward.

## Bores and Boring

Why is someone boring? Jumps and changes in conversation. The use and dangers of interruption. Diversions.

# DISCUSSION

This book is not about how to have an interesting conversation. There are people who are skilled at conversation but remain uninteresting people. They know how to lead a conversation and how to carry it forward but they do not know how to be interesting. This is an important distinction.

'Interest' is what happens in your mind and in the minds of others. Discussion allows you to present your thoughts; to listen to the thoughts of others; and to explore a subject jointly.

If you really have nothing at all to say then saying it very skilfully does not amount to much.

You need to develop the basic skill of 'interest' and you also need to know how to interact with others. Just as there are skilful conversationalists with nothing to say, there are also very interesting people with no skill at conversation. So the interest is not made available to others and is wasted.

There are three main components of a discussion:

1. Presenting, communicating and elaborating your own thinking and views on a subject.

2. Encouraging, building and developing a subject that is being presented by someone else or is in general discussion.

3. Leading out and prompting someone who is boring, to make that person less boring.

## Attention Directing

You choose to direct your attention to any part of the discussion. You can open up avenues or alleys of interest as you wish. You can extract concepts and play with them. Often some part of a boring subject is much more interesting than other parts. Changing the focus can revive a discussion that has become boring. If you sense an avenue of interest you can lead the others down it.

If you try one avenue and it does not work, then try another. There is a big difference between a scientific or business examination of a subject and a discussion. The purpose of the discussion is 'interest'. So you explore for interest and follow the interest. If this means that part of the subject gets insufficient attention that does not matter. If you are at a buffet dinner you do not have to take an equal serving of every dish offered. You choose what you want to eat. In exactly the same way you choose what interests you – and the others – in the discussion.

There is a need to develop a sensitivity as to whether a new avenue is working or not. Something may be of great interest to you but not to others. If you succeed in drawing others into your own interest then the avenue will work. If not, you had better try a different one.

Attention-directing is a bit like being a sheepdog. You note which way the sheep are heading and then you interact with them in order to get them to move forward. Sensitivity, suggestion and direction are the ways of leading a discussion to more interesting areas.

## Questions

Questions are a form of attention-directing, as suggested in an earlier section. The difference is that with a question you force others to direct their attention instead of just directing your own attention. Questions asked of oneself are a key component of 'interest'. Questions asked of other people are a key component of discussion.

# EXERCISE 62

What specific questions would you ask of other people in a discussion around the subject indicated below? These are not questions to yourself to open up the subject but specific questions to other people.

'In India, and some other countries, arranged marriages are common practice and even preferred. Many highly educated Indians prefer to follow this traditional custom. They feel that careful selection of a partner is better than the vagaries and fickleness of love. So the families and the marriage brokers arrange the match to suit temperament, background and business dynasties. If the person does not like the proposed partner there is always the option of rejection.'

In a discussion around this subject note down five questions which you could ask of others taking part in the discussion.

Do not turn to the next page until you have attempted this exercise

### *Exercise 62: Suggested Answers*

1. How would you feel about an arranged marriage for yourself?

2. Would you arrange a marriage for your children?

3. Why is an arranged marriage often considered to be less satisfactory than a 'love' marriage?

4. Do you think it is possible to 'fall in love' with an arranged partner?

5. Do you think a young person 'in love' is a better selector of a partner than the parents or an experienced marriage broker?

Questions need to be very specific. It is not much use asking a general question such as: 'What do you feel about . . . ?'

With a question you need to put someone on the spot. If that person does not want to answer or answers evasively, accept that response and do not pursue the matter. It is very boring to keep demanding an answer when the other person clearly does not want to give an answer.

## Speculations and Provocations

When the natural 'flow' of the discussion seems to have dried up, it can be useful to insert a speculation or a provocation to open up new alleys of interest. The nature and purpose of speculations and provocations have already been examined in a previous section. The listener is asked to think forward or 'run forward in the mind' from the starting-point given by the speculation.

# EXERCISE 63

What speculations or provocations might you offer to others in a discussion on the subject given below?

'In Japan married women are supposed to stay at home to look after the children, arrange their education and manage all the household finances. When they marry women in larger companies are expected to retire and stay at home.'

Note down five speculations on the subject.

---

Do not turn to the next page until you have attempted this exercise

---

## Exercise 63: Suggested Answers

1. Suppose it was required that any mother with children had to stay home to look after them. What would happen?

2. Po companies had to offer crèches and part-time work to mothers.

3. Po methods of working from home via computer were more fully developed.

4. Po everyone had two wives: a child-bearing wife and a companion wife.

5. Po men had to take two days a week off to look after the children.

# Alternatives and Choices

Interest can be stimulated by seeking alternatives and by offering a limited number of choices. In a way an offered choice is an attention-directing device. Instead of just asking someone to 'think' in general you provide the specific framework for the thinking. Some people are not good at open-ended thinking but are much better at reactive thinking. You ask someone to think about 'colour' and they get lost. Ask them to choose between 'red' and 'blue' and they might have a lot to think and to say.

You can also start off by offering some alternatives and then ask for additions to this list.

'To reduce traffic congestion in a city we could restrict cars or we could build better roads. What else might we do?'

'To increase employment we could provide more training or encourage investment. What else might we do?'

'To get better service in a hotel we could be more selective in our recruitment or offer better training. What else could we do?'

Vines grow along wires. Creepers climb over trellises. In the same way thinking often needs some framework. Speculations, provocations, alternatives and choices offer such frameworks. Instead of a vine shoot waving in the air there is a wire to guide it. Instead of free thinking with nowhere to go there is the offered framework.

# EXERCISE 64

In a discussion centred on the subject given below what five sets of choices might you put before the other people taking part in the discussion?

'Thinking is the most basic and most important of all human skills. Yet only rarely do we teach thinking directly and explicitly in schools. Even when we do so we often teach only critical thinking, which is a small part of thinking. It is true that there is no gap in the curriculum and that introduction of "thinking" would reduce time spent on other examination subjects. So few principals are willing to do it. There is also a belief that thinking cannot be taught but is simply a matter of inherited intelligence.'

Do not turn to the next page until you have attempted this exercise

## *Exercise 64: Suggested Answers*

1. Is thinking a skill which can be taught deliberately, or is thinking something which we pick up as we go through life?

2. Can thinking be taught directly or only as the by-product of teaching other material such as geography, mathematics, etc.

3. Are intelligent people automatically good thinkers or is thinking a separate skill?

4. Do we make specific space for thinking in the curriculum or do we put it in as part of some other subject, like language?

5. Which is the most important: getting through the examinations or developing life skills (such as thinking)?

The choices here have been put down as either/or. Often there can be more complex choices. The purpose of the offered choice is not to categorize people or their opinions but to open up thinking and discussion about the subject.

# Opinions

Offering an opinion is also a way of stimulating thinking in a discussion. As with the previous operations, an opinion offers a framework for thinking. People find it easier to think reactively rather than proactively. They find it easier to like or dislike a food dish put before them than to design a food dish. So offering an opinion invites people to:

1. Agree

2. Disagree

3. Suggest modifications or qualifications.

# EXERCISE 65

Suggest five different possible opinions that could be offered in a discussion around the following subject.

'There is designer mania. People have to wear designer clothes and bags and sunglasses. They write with designer pens and drink designer water. This may be to show their good taste or their level of spending. It may be that they have more faith in the choice of the designer than in their own. It may also be that since designers have a reputation to lose they demand higher standards of workmanship.'

---

Do not turn to the next page until you have attempted this exercise

---

## Exercise 65: Suggested Answers

1. People wearing designer labels do so just to show off.

2. People wear designer labels to join the 'club' of others who wear designer labels.

3. The quality of designer goods has to be higher to justify the higher price.

4. Why consent to be used as an unpaid billboard to advertise some designer's name?

5. Designer labels are a device to allow higher profit margins to be obtained.

It is possible to hold contradictory opinions and also parallel but different opinions. There is no real need to be consistent.

If you never change your mind – why have one?

## AGREEMENT

It is because most people do not know how to handle 'agreement' that they prefer 'disagreement'.

Agreement seems weak and uninteresting. You exert your ego, your importance and your presumed superiority through disagreement. Agreement seems sycophantic – you are inferior to the person with whom you agree because he 'owns' the opinion and you are just following.

If an economist woke up one morning and found that she or he agreed fully with another economist then that person is instantly superfluous.

Just as so many women do not know how to accept a compliment, so do most people not know how to offer agreement.

To disagree for the sake of disagreement is petty, stupid and the mark of a puny ego.

Unfortunately the famous Greek Gang of Three who wrecked Western thinking (Socrates, Plato and Aristotle) put forward the absurd notion that dialectic and argument were the methods to discover the 'truth'. I fully agree with this claim, but discovering the truth is only one small part of thinking. The productive, generative and creative part is much more important.

Agreement is encouragement. Why should we not make an attempt to encourage someone in their exploration of a subject? Why should it diminish our own importance to give importance to others?

# EXERCISE 66

In the following list of statements pick out those with which you strongly agree and those with which you agree – but less strongly.

1. It is not enough for 'greenies' to be against everything.

2. Less-developed countries may need to go through the 'polluting phase' which so benefited developing countries.

3. The environment is a global concern. What happens in any one country is everyone's business.

4. Providing employment and economic development may be more important than preserving the habitat of an owl.

5. There is a lot of scientific disagreement about the onset and consequences of the greenhouse effect.

6. Cows produce 70 million tonnes of methane a year and this is a very serious greenhouse gas. We should cut down on beef.

7. Children should be indoctrinated with ecological concerns at school so that they can then influence their parents.

8. No one who has enjoyed the benefits of pollution wants to pay for cleaning it up.

9. Things are getting steadily better.

10. Scare tactics are the only ones that work.

Do not turn to the next page until you have attempted this exercise

## Exercise 66: Suggested Answers

Strongly agree: 1, 3, 4, 5, 8

Agree: 9, 10

We need to develop a repertoire of ways of agreeing.

'I like that point . . .'

'I am in complete agreement with you on that . . .'

'That is a powerful concept . . .'

'That is also my own thinking . . .'

'I have come to the same conclusion . . .'

'Yes, that is important . . .'

# Develop and Build Upon

Agreement does not simply have to be passive acceptance. You should be making an effort to develop, to elaborate and to build upon the points with which you have agreed. You may want to give further examples. You may want to speak from your own experience. You may want to take the concept further than the person who offered it. Think of agreement as a starting-point.

# EXERCISE 67

The following five suggestions were made in a discussion on 'tourism'. Seek to add to or build upon each of the suggestions.

There should be:

1. A tourist telephone 'hotline' for complaints and another one for information.

2. Personal secretaries available for hire to smooth out both business and leisure activities.

3. Video cassettes sent in advance to advise on local customs and places to see.

4. An opportunity to report back after the holiday giving general impressions.

5. Ways of meeting local people.

---

Do not turn to the next page until you have attempted this exercise

---

## *Exercise 67: Suggested Answers*

1. There should also be some guarantee that the complaint would be followed up within a specified time – and some way of monitoring this.

2. Perhaps a general 'people' agency. Some might want babysitters, others might want a driver, or a guide, or a cook, etc.

3. These should be available for rental from tour companies and travel agencies. It should also be possible to view them on booths within the travel agency.

4. A follow-up sampling request with some reward for complying.

5. Local people could agree to be on a 'party list' and guests would be picked randomly from this list to attend receptions.

## **Partial Agreement**

There are times when agreement is not total. You may agree 'under certain circumstances' or 'if certain conditions are met'. You may agree with part of what is said or the general direction, but not with the specific idea.

At any time you can express such partial agreement. You do need to spell out very clearly indeed the qualifications or reservations that you have.

Every suggestion is complex and simple yes/no responses are rare. The expression of partial agreement is much better than having to disagree because you cannot fully agree.

# EXERCISE 68

If you partially agree with any of the following statements, indicate the nature of your agreement.

1. People should be penalized, by tax or otherwise, for not looking after their own health.

2. Foods which are not 'healthy' should all be packed in a bright yellow package.

3. There should be stand-alone terminals so people can diagnose their own ailments through structured questions.

4. There should be a grade of medical personnel below 'doctor' to deal with most straightforward conditions.

5. The profit margins on pharmaceuticals should be regulated individually.

6. Everyone should contribute some time to nursing or health care or pay a fee to be excused.

7. There should be standard kits of home-care equipment.

8. Facilities should be available for looking after old people at home.

9. All medical liability insurance should be carried by the government.

10. Second opinions should be readily available.

---

Do not turn to the next page until you have attempted this exercise

## *Exercise 68: Suggested Answers*

1. Yes, in principle, but almost impossible to do practically or fairly.

2. Some indication, but less fierce.

3. Only if the programmes were very good and foolproof. Otherwise much worry would be engendered in hypochondriacs.

4. Yes, with clear-cut training and title.

5. Only if provision was made to cover the cost of research into unsuccessful drugs.

6. Yes, as one option during a year of 'community service'; must not compete with the nursing profession as such.

7. Yes, if these were periodically monitored.

8. Would only be practical in some cases.

9. Yes, with a loading for doctors who are less competent.

10. Yes, but there is a danger of confusion.

# DISAGREEMENT

The only real role of negativity is to be negative about negativity.

In practice there are a whole number of reasons why people are negative:

... to be noticed
... to contribute and be involved
... to exercise their ego
... as part of a power-play attack on someone
... to demonstrate superiority
... because they have a different view
... because they cannot let an assertion go unchallenged
... because someone has the facts wrong
... because they believe argument is useful
... because it makes them feel important
... because they are aggressive
... because they like fights
... because they want to show how clever they are
... because they want to humiliate someone
... because everyone expects it from them.

The list could go on. It is obvious that many of the reasons for being negative have little to do with discovering the truth. Being negative is a pastime, a habit and a form of aggression. Most of all it is attention seeking and ego driven.

So what do we do in those genuine instances where there is a real disagreement?

## Parallel Thinking

Parallel thinking is very different from traditional adversarial thinking (see my book *Parallel Thinking*). In parallel thinking you do not seek to prove the other person wrong. Instead you lay down your view alongside the other view. It may be that both views are right.

There is the story of the man who painted half his car red and half grey because he liked to hear witnesses contradict each other when he was involved in a motor accident.

Genuine disagreement can arise from:

1. different information
2. looking at something from a different perspective
3. looking at a different part of the situation
4. different operating values
5. different extrapolations into the future.

All these differences are made much more apparent and much easier to see in parallel thinking than in traditional adversarial thinking.

# EXERCISE 69

For the following disagreement lay down in parallel the possible different views, information, values, experience and extrapolations involved.

(A) believes that youngsters in school should start to learn about the world outside: how shops function; how business works; what government is about; how people behave.

(B) believes that schools should stick to the traditional subjects of a general liberal education. Other things should be learned out of school or after leaving school.

Lay down the different possible views alongside each other at every point.

---

Do not turn to the next page until you have attempted this exercise

---

## *Exercise 69: Suggested Answers*

A. Feels that the purpose of education is to prepare youngsters to exist and work in the real world. There are things which youngsters should know and do not know.

(This is a matter of 'values' and 'purpose'.)

B. Sees this as 'utilitarian' education. He believes that liberal education should consist of developing the youngster and equipping the youngster with an understanding of civilization, particularly the past.

(A different value in the nature of education.)

A. Feels that unless education can be made more relevant youngsters will drop out and will not be prepared to work in the competitive global environment. The economical well-being of the country will decline.

(This is an extrapolation to the future.)

B. Believes that the suggestion is 'the thin end of the wedge'. More and more practical subjects will be introduced and the idea of a 'liberal' education will be lost. Society will be made up of working robots programmed only to work.

(A different extrapolation.)

A. Can quote figures from surveys showing that schoolchildren know remarkably little about the world around them. They may know the names of all the wives of King Henry the Eighth but not how the corner-shop works. There are also figures from industry suggesting that youngsters are not prepared for the workplace.

(Information background.)

B. Shows that many children spend more hours watching television than being in school. So why blame school?

(Different information.)

A. Believes that schools are out of date and are not keeping up

with the needs of a modern society. He believes that education is a locked-in, complacent and self-serving establishment which does not respond to the needs of society.
(A general feeling.)

B. Believes that schools should not change with every whim and fashion. The traditions of the past have served us very well. We should not abandon them. Change will happen slowly over time through evolution as it always has done.
(A general feeling.)

Laying out these differences in parallel makes it easy to see where the disagreement lies. The next stage would be to design a way forward.


## Arrogance

Surely it is necessary to attack 'arrogance' with its rigid views and sweeping generalizations based not on fact but on prejudice?

The best antidote to arrogance is the generation of alternatives. If someone insists that there is only one way to look at the situation, you present a possible alternative. If someone makes a sweeping generalization, you show exceptions. If someone insists on the validity of his or her fact, you ask where they came from and how they were obtained.

The comparison approach is more effective than head-on disagreement.

# EXERCISE 70

For each of the following arrogant statements lay down some alternatives.

1. 'Women are too emotional to be put in charge of anything important.'

2. 'Men are only concerned with their egos and not with what they are supposed to be managing.'

3. 'Low-paid foreign workers are taking the work from our own people.'

4. 'Free competition is the only way the economy can work.'

---

Do not turn to the next page until you have attempted this exercise

---

## Exercise 70: Suggested Answers

1. 'Many people have met men who are very emotional and women who are not.'
'It is possible to be emotional and also to be in control of your emotions.'
'Without emotions there are no values and no determination. Emotion is a good thing.'

2. 'Everyone has an ego. If you did not have an ego what would you have instead?'
'Men simply make less effort to hide their egos than women do.'
'There need not be any conflict between having an ego and managing. Many very successful entrepreneurs have huge egos.'

3. 'Automation decreases the cost of labour by increasing productivity.'
'If we are not competitive on costs then anyone can take our work.'
'Foreign workers also provide a market for our goods.'

4. 'Free competition on one side is not the same as free competition on both sides.'
'Free competition only works if everyone follows the rules.'
'Free competition is designed to look after the consumer but not to look after the worker.'

## Adjectives

Beware of anyone who uses too many adjectives. This is because adjectives are based on subjective feeling but are put forward as if they had a basis in fact. Disagreements are often based on no more than a disagreement with a choice of adjective. Vehemence is expressed through adjectives. Someone wants everyone to know that his or her feelings are deeply felt.

# EXERCISE 71

Below there is a list of adjectives and a list of people. The adjectives are jumbled up. Many of the adjectives might be used for many of the types of people. Sort them out to your taste and then, again, as you think most other people might sort them out.

| | |
|---|---|
| husbands | short-sighted |
| management | lazy |
| unemployed | blinkered |
| unions | naïve |
| children | greedy |
| wives | indifferent |

---

Do not turn to the next page until you have attempted this exercise

## *Exercise 71: Suggested Answers*

*Self*

husbands / naïve
management / blinkered
unemployed / short-sighted
unions / lazy
children / greedy
wives / indifferent

*Others*

husbands / indifferent
management / greedy
unemployed / naïve
unions / short-sighted
children / blinkered
wives / lazy

# Clarify and Map

Short of a designed outcome that accommodates different values and different fears, the most useful outcome is a clarification of the actual points of disagreement and a mapping of these. There is agreement to disagree on certain points. Some matters such as choice of values and extrapolations into the future are always open-ended and subjective. The intention of a designed outcome is to embrace the different points of view.

Just as a good map makes it much easier to decide which route to take, so the laying out of views, values, fears and needs makes it easier to design an outcome or to choose between alternatives.

# The Six Hats

As I indicated earlier, the Six Hats framework is becoming very widely used for discussions. It is a complete contrast to traditional adversarial argument. It is an effective method for parallel thinking. Meeting times are much reduced. Fuller use is made of the intelligence and experience of those taking part in the discussion. Ego-based thinking has no place. Instead of the macho defence of an idea or attack upon another idea there is cooperative exploration. Major corporations around the world are rapidly taking it up because traditional 'Gang of Three' thinking was never designed to be constructive. Indeed, Western civilization has never developed an idiom of constructive thinking.

At each moment in a Six Hats meeting everyone is wearing the same coloured hat. There is no argument. Ideas are put down in parallel. The white hat is for information – of any sort. The red hat asks for feelings, intuitions and emotions – without any need to justify them. The black hat is for caution and risk assessment – why something may not work. The yellow hat is for seeking out benefits and values – the logical positive hat. The green hat is for creativity, possibilities, alternatives and new ideas – the energy hat. The blue hat is for managing the thinking process – like the conductor of an orchestra.

Although the method seems simple and is simple, the best effects are obtained when there has been some thorough training in the method. (For information see p.289.)

With the Six Hats method disagreements dissolve and disappear. The emphasis is not on 'battle' but on designing the way forward. At the end of the Six Hats session the decision has usually made itself.

# BORES AND BORING

A good bore is a work of art. You marvel that anyone could be so boring and not ever notice it.

A bore is a monologue. Except on a 'twosome' basis, someone who has nothing to say is rarely a bore.

Some clever people end up being bores when they have the potential to be very interesting. Such people lay their thoughts before you just as they might give you a book and say, 'Read this.'

It is not that a bore has no interest in his or her listeners. There is no sensitivity to the reaction of the listeners and no consideration that it is possible to be boring.

Like all other forms of arrogance being a bore is a form of bullying.

Unless your story is totally new or exceptionally fascinating, you are a bore if you are not interrupted. If interruptions do not come then you need to stimulate them. Pause to ask questions. Pause to see if your listeners are at all interested. Almost any subject can be made interesting through possibilities, speculation, elaboration and questions.

When you see a glimmer of interest in the eyes of the listener seek to build on that. If there is no such glimmer continue to try different approaches to the subject. Pull in some of the basic human-interest drivers. You can personalize and emphasize relevance. You can also try 'humenes' with surprises and insights. But you have to want to. Mostly, bores do not see any need to do anything other than to continue to bore. Do bores know they are boring? Some do and some do not.

# EXERCISE 72

Of the six subjects listed below consider which might be the three most boring and which the three more interesting ones.

1. Athletics, physical fitness and training.

2. Handwriting analysis and character indication.

3. Holidays in general (not a specific one). Likes, dislikes and choices of places to go.

4. Twins. The behaviour of twins.

5. Frogs – nature, behaviour.

6. Glass – ornamental, windows, drinking vessels.

---

Do not turn to the next page until you have attempted this exercise

---

## *Exercise 72: Suggested Answers*

Your choice will depend on the special knowledge you have of a subject and also on your personal interest. One set of choices might be.

### More boring

*Athletics:* more of a special interest. Not much to develop for those who do not have this special interest.

*Holidays:* possible to get a lot of information. The subject is so very wide that a great deal can be said with none of it being interesting. Too easy a subject.

*Frogs:* unless you have a special knowledge it requires a lot of skill to bring out what is potentially a very interesting subject – but a difficult one.

### More interesting

*Handwriting analysis:* personal because everyone has his or her own handwriting. Does this really depend on character? Use of handwriting analysis in business. Most people know outstanding personalities with poor handwriting – and the other way around. An involving subject.

*Twins:* always an interesting subject. Numerous stories of transmitting their thoughts and feelings, getting sick on the same day, etc. Involving notions of being both different and yet the same.

*Glass:* wide subject ranging from domestic glass to glass as an art form. Intriguing that such a simple substance as sand can be turned into something so beautiful. Contrast with gold and silver which start off as such and are expensive. One of the most powerful transformations of value: sand into glass and glass into a work of art.

## Jumps

When should the subject be changed? At what point should there be a jump? Should the jump be sharp and noticeable or a smooth transition which no one notices?

Everyone taking part in a conversation or a discussion has a responsibility to change the subject if the current subject is becoming boring. Should you change the subject or try to inject new life into the existing subject through speculation and provocation? If the subject is changed every time it flags then there will be a sort of random dance in which no subject is ever explored for long enough for it to be interesting. So the first effort should always be to get more interest out of the existing subject. When that has been tried and has succeeded, or failed, then it is time to change the subject.

The transition can be made through a concept, through personal experience or through special information.

It is not enough just to change the subject. The new subject must be set on an 'interest course' through opening up avenues of interest. Whoever changes the subject has the duty to do that. It is not much use just dumping a new subject before others and asking them to make it interesting.

# EXERCISE 73

Below are given three pairs of subjects. For each pair suggest how you might make a smooth transition from discussing the first subject to discussing the second one.

1. from 'good food' to 'book'
2. from 'insurance' to 'music'
3. from 'cartoons' to 'carpets'.

---

Do not turn to the next page until you have attempted this exercise

## *Exercise 73: Suggested Answers*

1. Through the matter of 'writing about food'. Can words adequately describe tastes and sensation? Is a word-picture much use in describing food? And so on to books and descriptions of things. Another route might be through the large number of cookbooks that are published and bought.

2. Insurance is about something that may or may not happen in the future. Life is about what may or may not happen in the future. There is flow and expectation. That is also the nature of music. What comes next? What is signalled ahead? How much should music hint at what is to follow? Themes are suggested and then picked up later.

3. Cartoons are really 'concept designs'. The concepts are 'figurative' in the sense that they deal with people and people's behaviour. There are not many things in ordinary life that are 'concept designs'. Carpets are one of them. But the concepts are abstract and geometrical rather than figurative. Carpets are like visual music.

# Interrupt

There is a story about an Italian professor who was so very busy that he would commence his lecture and then place a tape recorder on his desk and go away to do his work. The tape recorder would deliver the rest of his lecture. One day he came back unexpectedly early. To his surprise there were no students in the hall. Instead there were tape recorders on each desk, listening to his tape recorder.

Interruptions are a necessary part of interaction and interest. Without interruptions there is a lecture. With interruptions there is a conversation.

Interruptions can be a nuisance when:

... they interrupt the flow of a story at the wrong moment

... when they are too frequent

... when they introduce an irrelevant diversion.

... when they are of the ego-driven 'notice me' type.

An interruption may ask a question; insert new information; insert personal experience; insert personal feeling; ask for clarification; and redefine the subject-matter.

# EXERCISE 74

There is a rather boring discussion about traffic congestion and the difficulty of driving in a city.

Suggest four different interruptions that you might make to liven things up.

## *Exercise 74: Suggested Answers*

1. Special information: 'In London the average speed of a car is four miles an hour and the average speed of a bicycle is eight miles an hour.'

2. Provocation: 'Po everyone could be a taxi, as in Peru, so you never need to drive yourself. You can sit and read.'

3. Choice: 'Would you rather work at home via a computer link or face the hassle of driving in to work but enjoying the company of others?'

4. Speculation: 'If traffic is allowed to get really bad will it eventually sort itself out because people will not want to use their own cars? Perhaps the right policy is to do nothing at all. In fact you might dig more holes in the road to accelerate the "fed-up" process.'

# Diversions

If you introduce a deliberate diversion it is up to you to lead the subject back to where it was – unless you intended your diversion as a 'jump'.

It is boring for someone to introduce a diversion and then leave things hanging in the air. It is just like those road signs that signal a diversion to get traffic off the main road and then forget all about the traffic, leaving it to find its own way back to the main road.

# PART 5
# SUMMARY

# SUMMARY

This book is about 'interest'. Interest is what happens in your mind.

A good cook can make an excellent meal out of few or poor ingredients. Interest is the same sort of skill as cooking. How do you treat the information or experience that you have? How do you put things together? Just as there are basic operations of cooking so there are also basic operations of 'interest' such as: possibilities, speculations, provocations, concept extraction, etc. These basic operations are covered in this book.

A cook knows how to add flavour. In terms of interest flavour takes the form of feelings, emotions, personal experience, relevance and the 'humenes'.

You can become more interesting if you set out to do so. Like riding a bicycle it may seem awkward at first. Then it becomes easier and easier. Like riding a bicycle it may seem 'artificial'. Why not just exist, breathe, talk and experience? There would be no art at all if people just sat around 'being'. Art is artificial.

Being an interesting person means that you are more interesting to yourself as well as to others. Life becomes more interesting. Other people become more interesting.

This book is not about how to be a skilled conversationalist. That is not the same as being interesting. Some skilled conversationalists are not interesting. But if you are interesting in yourself then your conversation is likely to be more interesting.

So it is not enough to be healthy, fit and beautiful. Why not have a beautiful mind as well? Your mind is going to be with you until you die. It need not age at all.

Bores are predictable. Some boring critic is going to write that this is a boring book on being interesting. It may be if you read it that way.

# INFORMATION

From time to time readers request further information regarding materials and courses based on the work of Edward de Bono, both in the area of education and also of business. As a help to readers contact information is given here.

## Internet
(for comprehensive details on courses, etc.)

http://www.edwdebono.com./

http://www/edwdebono.co.uk

http://www/edwdebono,aust.com

## Business Training Courses

1. Six thinking Hats

2. Lateral Thinking

3. DATT (Direct Attention Thinking Tools)

*UK:* tel. 01494 866971
fax. 01494 868787

*Australia:* tel. 03 9614 5277
fax. 03 9614 5344

*USA:* tel. (515) 278 5570
fax. (515) 278 2245

*Ireland:* tel. 01 8250 466
fax. 01 825 0467

## *Education Programmes for Schools*

The CoRT Programme (60 lessons)

Six Thinking Hats

Think Note Write

For all these please contact the numbers given above.

For Edward de Bono please fax (UK): 0171 602 1779.

# ABOUT THE AUTHOR

Edward de Bono is widely acknowledged as a leading figure in thinking about thinking. He is the originator of lateral thinking, which is now part of everyday language. He has written fifty-seven books, which have been translated into thirty-four languages, and has been invited to lecture in fifty-eight countries. There are more than four million references to his work on the Internet. There is also a minor planet named after him.

Edward de Bono was the first to show how the self-organizing nature of the human brain gives rise to humour and demands creativity. He has insisted that the traditional Western thinking idioms designed by the Gang of Three (Socrates, Plato and Aristotle) are insufficient in a changing world where judgement alone is not enough. We need the skills of constructive thinking, creative thinking and design thinking.

Edward de Bono was a Rhodes Scholar at Oxford and has held appointments at the universities of Oxford, Cambridge, London and Harvard.

# EDWARD DE BONO

**LATERAL THINKING: A TEXTBOOK OF CREATIVITY**

In schools we are taught to meet problems head-on: what Edward de Bono calls 'vertical thinking'. This works well in simple situations – but we are at a loss when this approach fails. What then?

Lateral thinking is all about freeing up your imagination. Through a series of special techniques, in groups or working alone, Edward de Bono shows how to stimulate the mind in new and exciting ways.

Soon you will be looking at problems from a variety of angles and offering up solutions that are as ingenious as they are effective. You will become much more productive and a formidable thinker in your own right.

# EDWARD DE BONO

## I AM RIGHT, YOU ARE WRONG

Most of our everyday decision-making tends to be confrontational. Whether in large meetings, one-to-one or even in our own heads, opposite view points are pitted against each other. Ultimately, there must be a winner and a loser.

In *I Am Right, You Are Wrong,* lateral-thinking guru Edward de Bono challenges this 'rock logic' of rigid categories and point-scoring arguments which is both destructive and exhausting.

Instead he reveals how we can all be winners. Clearer perception is the key to constructive thinking and more open-minded creativity. In overturning conventional wisdom, Edward de Bono will help you to become a better thinker and decision maker.

# EDWARD DE BONO

## TEACH YOUR CHILD HOW TO THINK

The greatest gift we can give our children is the ability to think for themselves. Unfortunately, this is not something that can be learned at school or from any child's friends or peers. Only a parent may teach it.

Edward de Bono, the lateral-thinking pioneer, shows in a simple and practical way how any parent can develop the thinking skills of their children. This is not about winning arguments, learning facts or articulation, but about constructive thinking, making the right choices and decisions, planning and creativity.

This book gives invaluable techniques for coping with the many problems and opportunities that lie in wait for your child. It might just be the best start you can give them in life.

# EDWARD DE BONO

**TEACH YOURSELF TO THINK**

Our happiness and success depend on clear thinking. But too many of us are compromised by confusion, trying to do too much at once, and not knowing what to do next.

In *Teach Yourself to Think*, Edward de Bono shows that good thinking depends on a simple five-stage process that anyone can learn. It will enable you to assess your goals, sort available information, identify the available choices, make a decision and, finally, turn thought into action.

This book offers brilliant advice for anyone who needs to be able to respond to and deal with a vast range of situations at work and in life quickly, efficiently and intelligently.

# EDWARD DE BONO

## SIMPLICITY

From confusing manuals to uninterpretable jargon and bureaucratic red-tape, modern life can be highly complicated and frustrating. For many of us it is almost impossible to make sense of.

In *Simplicity*, lateral-thinking guru Edward de Bono shows us how to bring clarity into our increasingly complicated lives. Through his ten rules of simplicity, he encourages us to be creative and break down the complex into manageable and recognisable parts.

By making the complicated simple, you will free up time, reduce stress and make better decisions.

# EDWARD DE BONO

**SIX THINKING HATS**

Meetings are a crucial part of all our lives, but too often they go nowhere and waste valuable time. In *Six Thinking Hats*, Edward de Bono shows how meetings can be transformed to produce quick, decisive results every time.

The Six Hats method is a devastatingly simple technique based on the brain's different modes of thinking. The intelligence, experience and information of everyone is harnessed to reach the right conclusions quickly.

These principles fundamentally change the way you work and interact. They have been adopted by businesses and governments around the world to end conflict and confusion in favour of harmony and productivity.

# He just wanted a decent book to read ...

Not too much to ask, is it? It was in 1935 when Allen Lane, Managing Director of Bodley Head Publishers, stood on a platform at Exeter railway station looking for something good to read on his journey back to London. His choice was limited to popular magazines and poor-quality paperbacks – the same choice faced every day by the vast majority of readers, few of whom could afford hardbacks. Lane's disappointment and subsequent anger at the range of books generally available led him to found a company – and change the world.

*'We believed in the existence in this country of a vast reading public for intelligent books at a low price, and staked everything on it'*
**Sir Allen Lane, 1902–1970, founder of Penguin Books**

The quality paperback had arrived – and not just in bookshops. Lane was adamant that his Penguins should appear in chain stores and tobacconists, and should cost no more than a packet of cigarettes.

Reading habits (and cigarette prices) have changed since 1935, but Penguin still believes in publishing the best books for everybody to enjoy. We still believe that good design costs no more than bad design, and we still believe that quality books published passionately and responsibly make the world a better place.

So wherever you see the little bird – whether it's on a piece of prize-winning literary fiction or a celebrity autobiography, political tour de force or historical masterpiece, a serial-killer thriller, reference book, world classic or a piece of pure escapism – you can bet that it represents the very best that the genre has to offer.

## Whatever you like to read – trust Penguin.